For my family

Contents

POEMS 1965–1975

From THE CIRCLE GAME

From THE ANIMALS IN THAT COUNTRY

From POWER POLITICS

Acknowledgements

Grateful acknowledgement is made for permission to reprint from the following:

Poems from *The Animals in That Country*, by Margaret Atwood, copyright © 1968 by Oxford University Press (Canadian Branch) and poems from *Procedures for Underground*, by Margaret Atwood, copyright © 1970 by Oxford University Press (Canadian Branch) by permission of Little, Brown and Co. in association with the Atlantic Monthly Press.

Poems from *The Journals of Susanna Moodie*, copyright © 1976 by Oxford University Press, by permission of Oxford University Press.

Poems from *You Are Happy* by Margaret Atwood, copyright © 1974 by Margaret Atwood by permission of Harper & Row, Publishers, Inc.

Poems from *Power Politics* by Margaret Atwood, copyright © 1971 by Margaret Atwood. Poems from *The Circle Game*, copyright © 1966 by Margaret Atwood. Reprinted by permission of the House of Anansi Press.

Grateful acknowledgement is made to Jonathan Cape Ltd for permission to publish poems from *True Stories* (1982) and *Interlunar* (1984).

Grateful acknowledgement is made to the following where some of these poems have appeared:

The Atlantic Monthly, *Carnage Hall Magazine*, *Field*, *Harper's*, *Islands of Hope* (Firefly Books), *The Michigan Quarterly Review*, *Mississippi Valley Review*, *New Letters*, *The Paris Review*, *Ploughshares*, *River Styx*, *This Magazine*, *The Times Literary Supplement* and *vice Versa*.

Poems

1965–1975

From

The Circle Game

1966

THIS IS A PHOTOGRAPH OF ME

It was taken some time ago.
At first it seems to be
a smeared
print: blurred lines and grey flecks
blended with the paper;

then, as you scan
it, you see in the left-hand corner
a thing that is like a branch: part of a tree
(balsam or spruce) emerging
and, to the right, halfway up
what ought to be a gentle
slope, a small frame house.

In the background there is a lake,
and beyond that, some low hills.

(The photograph was taken
the day after I drowned.

I am in the lake, in the center
of the picture, just under the surface.

It is difficult to say where
precisely, or to say
how large or small I am:
the effect of water
on light is a distortion

but if you look long enough,
eventually
you will be able to see me.)

AFTER THE FLOOD, WE

We must be the only ones
left, in the mist that has risen
everywhere as well
as in these woods

I walk across the bridge
towards the safety of high ground
(the tops of the trees are like islands)

gathering the sunken
bones of the drowned mothers
(hard and round in my hands)
while the white mist washes
around my legs like water;

fish must be swimming
down in the forest beneath us,
like birds, from tree to tree
and a mile away
the city, wide and silent,
is lying lost, far undersea.

You saunter beside me, talking
of the beauty of the morning,
not even knowing
that there has been a flood,

tossing small pebbles
at random over your shoulder
into the deep thick air,

not hearing the first stumbling
footsteps of the almost-born

coming (slowly) behind us,
not seeing
the almost-human
brutal faces forming
(slowly)
out of stone.

THE CITY PLANNERS

Cruising these residential Sunday
streets in dry August sunlight:
what offends us is
the sanities:
the houses in pedantic rows, the planted
sanitary trees, assert
levelness of surface like a rebuke
to the dent in our car door.
No shouting here, or
shatter of glass; nothing more abrupt
than the rational whine of a power mower
cutting a straight swath in the discouraged grass.

But though the driveways neatly
sidestep hysteria
by being even, the roofs all display
the same slant of avoidance to the hot sky,
certain things:
the smell of spilled oil a faint
sickness lingering in the garages,
a splash of paint on brick surprising as a bruise,
a plastic hose poised in a vicious
coil; even the too-fixed stare of the wide windows

give momentary access to
the landscape behind or under
the future cracks in the plaster

when the houses, capsized, will slide
obliquely into the clay seas, gradual as glaciers
that right now nobody notices.

That is where the City Planners
with the insane faces of political conspirators
are scattered over unsurveyed
territories, concealed from each other,
each in his own private blizzard;

guessing directions, they sketch
transitory lines rigid as wooden borders
on a wall in the white vanishing air

tracing the panic of suburb
order in a bland madness of snows.

THE CIRCLE GAME

i

The children on the lawn
joined hand to hand
go round and round

each arm going into
the next arm, around
full circle
until it comes
back into each of the single
bodies again

They are singing, but
not to each other:
their feet move
almost in time to the singing

We can see
the concentration on
their faces, their eyes
fixed on the empty
moving spaces just in
front of them.

We might mistake this
tranced moving for joy
but there is no joy in it

We can see (arm in arm)
as we watch them go
round and round
intent, almost
studious (the grass
underfoot ignored, the trees
circling the lawn
ignored, the lake ignored)
that the whole point
for them
of going round and round
is (faster
            slower)
going round and round

ii

Being with you
here, in this room

is like groping through a mirror
whose glass has melted
to the consistency
of gelatin

You refuse to be
(and I)
an exact reflection, yet
will not walk from the glass,
be separate.

Anyway, it is right
that they have put
so many mirrors here
(chipped, hung crooked)
in this room with its high transom
and empty wardrobe; even
the back of the door
has one.

There are people in the next room
arguing, opening and closing drawers
(the walls are thin)

You look past me, listening
to them, perhaps, or
watching
your own reflection somewhere
behind my head,
over my shoulder

You shift, and the bed
sags under us, losing its focus

there is someone in the next room

there is always

(your face
remote, listening)

someone in the next room.

iii

However,
in all their games
there seems
to be some reason

however
abstract they
at first appear

When we read them legends
in the evening
of monstrous battles, and secret
betrayals in the forest
and brutal deaths,

they scarcely listened;
one yawned and fidgeted; another
chewed the wooden handle
of a hammer;
the youngest one examined
a slight cut on his toe,

and we wondered how
they could remain
completely without fear
or even interest
as the final sword slid through
the dying hero.

The next night
walking along the beach

we found the trenches
they had been making:
fortified with pointed sticks
driven into the sides
of their sand moats

and a lake-enclosed island
with no bridges:

a last attempt
(however
eroded by the water
in an hour)
to make
maybe, a refuge human
and secure from the reach

of whatever walks along
(sword hearted)
these night beaches.

iv

Returning to the room:
I notice how
all your word-
plays, calculated ploys
of the body, the witticisms
of touch, are now
attempts to keep me
at a certain distance
and (at length) avoid
admitting I am here

I watch you
watching my face
indifferently
yet with the same taut curiosity
with which you might regard
a suddenly discovered part
of your own body:
a wart perhaps,

and I remember that
you said
in childhood you were
a tracer of maps
(not making but) moving
a pen or a forefinger

over the courses of the rivers,
the different colours
that mark the rise of mountains;
a memorizer
of names (to hold
these places
in their proper places)

So now you trace me
like a country's boundary
or a strange new wrinkle in
your own wellknown skin
and I am fixed, stuck
down on the outspread map
of this room, of your mind's continent
        (here and yet not here, like
        the wardrobe and the mirrors
        the voices through the wall
        your body ignored on the bed),

transfixed
by your eyes'
cold blue thumbtacks

v

The children like the block
of grey stone that was once a fort
but now is a museum:

especially
they like the guns
and the armour brought from
other times and countries

and when they go home
their drawings will be full
for some days, of swords
archaic sunburst maces
broken spears
and vivid red explosions.

While they explore
the cannons
(they aren't our children)

we walk outside along
the earthworks, noting
how they are crumbling
under the unceasing
attacks of feet and flower roots;

The weapons
that were once outside
sharpening themselves on war
are now indoors
there, in the fortress,
fragile
in glass cases;

Why is it
(I'm thinking
of the careful moulding
round the stonework archways)
that in this time, such
elaborate defences keep
things that are no longer
(much)
worth defending?

vi

And you play the safe game
the orphan game

the ragged winter game
that says, I am alone

(hungry: I know you want me
to play it also)

the game of the waif who stands
at every picture window,

shivering, pinched nose pressed
against the glass, the snow
collecting on his neck,
watching the happy families

(a game of envy)

Yet he despises them: they are so
Victorian Christmas-card:
the cheap paper shows
under the pigments of
their cheerful fire-
places and satin-
ribboned suburban laughter
and they have their own forms
of parlour
games: father and mother
playing father and mother

He's glad
to be left
out by himself
in the cold

(hugging himself)

When I tell you this,
you say (with a smile fake
as a tinsel icicle):

You do it too.

Which in some ways
is a lie, but also I suppose
is right, as usual:

although I tend to pose
in other seasons
outside other windows.

vii

Summer again;
in the mirrors of this room
the children wheel, singing
the same song;

This casual bed
scruffy as dry turf,
the counterpane
rumpled with small burrows, is
their grassy lawn

and these scuffed walls
contain their circling trees,
that low clogged sink
their lake

(a wasp comes,
drawn by the piece of sandwich
left on the nearby beach
                    (how carefully you do
                    such details);
one of the children flinches
but won't let go)

You make them
turn and turn, according to
the closed rules of your games,
but there is no joy in it

and as we lie
arm in arm, neither
joined nor separate
        (your observations change me
        to a spineless woman in
        a cage of bones, obsolete fort
        pulled inside out),
our lips moving
almost in time to their singing,

listening to the opening
and closing of the drawers
in the next room

(of course there is always
danger but where
would you locate it)

(the children spin
a round cage of glass
from the warm air
with their thread-thin
insect voices)

and as we lie
here, caught
in the monotony of wandering
from room to room, shifting
the place of our defences,

I want to break
these bones, your prisoning rhythms
        (winter,
        summer)
all the glass cases,

erase all maps,
crack the protecting
eggshell of your turning
singing children:

I want the circle
broken.

JOURNEY TO THE INTERIOR

There are similarities
I notice: that the hills
which the eyes make flat as a wall, welded
together, open as I move
to let me through; become
endless as prairies; that the trees
grow spindly, have their roots
often in swamps; that this is a poor country;
that a cliff is not known
as rough except by hand, and is
therefore inaccessible. Mostly
that travel is not the easy going
from point to point, a dotted
line on a map, location
plotted on a square surface
but that I move surrounded by a tangle
of branches, a net of air and alternate
light and dark, at all times;
that there are no destinations
apart from this.

There are differences
of course: the lack of reliable charts;
more important, the distraction of small details:
your shoe among the brambles under the chair
where it shouldn't be; lucent

white mushrooms and a paring knife
on the kitchen table; a sentence
crossing my path, sodden as a fallen log
I'm sure I passed yesterday
                                        (have I been
walking in circles again?)

but mostly the danger:
many have been here, but only
some have returned safely.

A compass is useless; also
trying to take directions
from the movements of the sun,
which are erratic;
and words here are as pointless
as calling in a vacant
wilderness.
                Whatever I do I must
keep my head. I know
it is easier for me to lose my way
forever here, than in other landscapes

SOME OBJECTS OF WOOD AND STONE

i Totems

We went to the park
where they kept the wooden people:
static, multiple
uprooted and trans-
planted.

Their faces were restored,
freshly-painted.
In front of them

the other wooden people
posed for each other's cameras
and nearby a new booth
sold replicas and souvenirs.

One of the people was real.
It lay on its back, smashed
by a toppling fall or just
the enduring of minor winters.
Only one of the heads had
survived intact, and it was
also beginning to decay
but there was a
life in the progressing
of old wood back to
the earth, obliteration

that the clear-hewn
standing figures lacked.

As for us, perennial watchers,
tourists of another kind
there is nothing for us to worship;
no pictures of ourselves, no blue-
sky summer fetishes, no postcards
we can either buy, or
smiling
be.

There are few totems that remain
living for us.
Though in passing,
through glass we notice

dead trees in the seared meadows
dead roots bleaching in the swamps.

ii Pebbles

Talking was difficult. Instead
we gathered coloured pebbles
from the places on the beach
where they occurred.

They were sea-smoothed, sea-completed.
They enclosed what they intended
to mean in shapes
as random and necessary
as the shapes of words

and when finally
we spoke
the sounds of our voices fell
into the air   single and
solid and rounded and really
there
and then dulled, and then like sounds
gone,   a fistful of gathered
pebbles there was no point
in taking home, dropped on a beachful
of other coloured pebbles

and when we turned to go
a flock of small
birds flew scattered by the
fright of our sudden moving
and disappeared: hard

sea pebbles
thrown solid for an instant
against the sky

flight of words

iii Carved Animals

The small carved
animal is passed from
hand to hand
around the circle
until the stone grows warm

touching, the hands do not know
the form of animal
which was made or
the true form of stone
uncovered

and the hands, the fingers the
hidden small bones
of the hands bend to hold the shape,
shape themselves, grow
cold with the stone's cold, grow
also animal, exchange
until the skin wonders
if stone is human

In the darkness later
and even when the animal
has gone, they keep
the image of that
inner shape

hands holding warm
hands holding
the half-formed air

AGAINST STILL LIFE

Orange in the middle of a table:

It isn't enough
to walk around it
at a distance, saying
it's an orange:
nothing to do
with us, nothing
else: leave it alone

I want to pick it up
in my hand
I want to peel the
skin off; I want
more to be said to me
than just Orange:
want to be told
everything it has to say

And you, sitting across
the table, at a distance, with
your smile contained, and like the orange
in the sun: silent:

Your silence
isn't enough for me
now, no matter with what
contentment you fold
your hands together; I want
anything you can say
in the sunlight:

stories of your various
childhoods, aimless journeyings,
your loves; your articulate
skeleton; your posturings; your lies.

These orange silences
(sunlight and hidden smile)
make me want to
wrench you into saying;
now I'd crack your skull
like a walnut, split it like a pumpkin
to make you talk, or get
a look inside

But quietly:
if I take the orange
with care enough and hold it
gently

I may find
an egg
a sun
an orange moon
perhaps a skull; centre
of all energy
resting in my hand

can change it to
whatever I desire
it to be

and you, man, orange afternoon
lover, wherever
you sit across from me
(tables, trains, buses)

if I watch
quietly enough
and long enough

at last, you will say
(maybe without speaking)

(there are mountains
inside your skull
garden and chaos, ocean
and hurricane; certain
corners of rooms, portraits
of great-grandmothers, curtains
of a particular shade;
your deserts; your private
dinosaurs; the first
woman)

all I need to know:
tell me
everything
just as it was
from the beginning.

A PLACE: FRAGMENTS

i

Here on the rim, cringing
under the cracked whip of winter
we live
in houses of ice,
but not because we want to:
in order to survive
we make what we can and have to
with what we have.

ii

Old woman I visited once
out of my way
in a little-visited province:

she had a neat
house, a clean parlour
though obsolete and poor:

a cushion with a fringe;
glass animals arranged
across the mantelpiece (a swan, a horse,
a bull); a mirror;
a teacup sent from Scotland:
several heraldic spoons;
a lamp; and in the centre
of the table, a paperweight:
hollow glass globe
filled with water, and
a house, a man, a snowstorm.

The room was as
dustless as possible
and free of spiders.
I
stood in the door-
way, at the fulcrum where

this trivial but
stringent inner order
held its delicate balance
with the random scattering or
clogged merging of
things: ditch by the road; dried
reeds in the wind; flat
wet bush, grey sky
sweeping away outside.

iii

The cities are only outposts.

Watch that man
walking on cement as though on snowshoes:

senses the road
a muskeg, loose mat of roots and brown
vegetable decay
or crust of ice that
easily might break and
slush or water under
suck him down

The land flows like a
sluggish current.

The mountains eddy slowly towards the sea.

iv

The people who come here also
flow: their bodies becoming
nebulous, diffused, quietly
spreading out into the air across
these interstellar sidewalks

v

This is what it must be
like in outer space
where the stars are pasted flat
against the total
black of the expanding
eye, fly-
specks of burning dust

vi

There is no centre;
the centres
travel with us unseen
like our shadows
on a day when there is no sun.

We must move back:
there are too many foregrounds.

Now, clutter of twigs
across our eyes, tatter
of birds at the eye's edge; the straggle
of dead treetrunks; patch
of lichen
and in love, tangle
of limbs and fingers, the texture
of pores and lines on the skin.

vii

An other sense tugs at us:
we have lost something,
some key to these things
which must be writings
and are locked against us
or perhaps (like a potential
mine, unknown vein
of metal in the rock)
something not lost or hidden
but just not found yet

that informs, holds together
this confusion, this largeness
and dissolving:

not above or behind
or within it, but one
with it: an

identity:
something too huge and simple
for us to see.

THE EXPLORERS

The explorers will come
in several minutes
and find this island.

(It is a stunted island,
rocky, with room
for only a few trees, a thin
layer of soil; hardly
bigger than a bed.
That is how
they've missed it
until now)

Already their boats draw near,
their flags flutter,
their oars push at the water.

They will be jubilant
and shout, at finding
that there was something
they had not found before,

although this island will afford
not much more than a foothold:
little to explore;

but they will be surprised

(we can't see them yet;
we know they must be
coming, because they always come
several minutes too late)

(they won't be able
to tell how long
we were cast away, or why,
or, from these
gnawed bones,
which was the survivor)

at the two skeletons

THE SETTLERS

A second after
the first boat touched the shore,
there was a quick skirmish
brief as a twinge
and then the land was settled

(of course there was really
no shore: the water turned
to land by having
objects in it: caught and kept
from surge, made
less than immense
by networks of
roads and grids of fences)

and as for us, who drifted
picked by the sharks
during so many bluegreen
centuries before they came:
they found us
inland, stranded
on a ridge of bedrock,
defining our own island.

From our inarticulate
skeleton (so
intermixed, one
carcass),
they postulated wolves.

They dug us down
into the solid granite
where our bones grew flesh again,
came up trees and
grass.

Still
we are the salt
seas that uphold these lands.

Now horses graze
inside this fence of ribs, and

children run, with green
smiles, (not knowing
where) across
the fields of our open hands.

From

The Animals in That Country

1968

THE ANIMALS IN THAT COUNTRY

In that country the animals
have the faces of people:

the ceremonial
cats possessing the streets

the fox run
politely to earth, the huntsmen
standing around him, fixed
in their tapestry of manners

the bull, embroidered
with blood and given
an elegant death, trumpets, his name
stamped on him, heraldic brand
because

(when he rolled
on the sand, sword in his heart, the teeth
in his blue mouth were human)

he is really a man

even the wolves, holding resonant
conversations in their
forests thickened with legend.

> In this country the animals
> have the faces of
> animals.
>
> Their eyes
> flash once in car headlights
> and are gone.

Their deaths are not elegant.

They have the faces of
no-one.

THE LANDLADY

This is the lair of the landlady.

She is
a raw voice
loose in the rooms beneath me,

the continuous henyard
squabble going on below
thought in this house like
the bicker of blood through the head.

She is everywhere, intrusive as the smells
that bulge in under my doorsill;
she presides over my
meagre eating, generates
the light for eyestrain.
From her I rent my time:
she slams
my days like doors.
Nothing is mine

and when I dream images
of daring escapes through the snow
I find myself walking
always over a vast face
which is the land-
lady's, and wake up shouting.

She is a bulk, a knot
swollen in space. Though I have tried
to find some way around
her, my senses
are cluttered by perception
and can't see through her.

She stands there, a raucous fact
blocking my way:
immutable, a slab
of what is real,

solid as bacon.

AT THE TOURIST CENTRE IN BOSTON

There is my country under glass,
a white relief-
map with red dots for the cities,
reduced to the size of a wall

and beside it 10 blownup snapshots
one for each province,
in purple-browns and odd reds,
the green of the trees dulled;
all blues however
of an assertive purity.

Mountains and lakes and more lakes
(though Quebec is a restaurant and Ontario the empty
interior of the parliament buildings),
with nobody climbing the trails and hauling out
the fish and splashing in the water

but arrangements of grinning tourists –
look here, Saskatchewan

is a flat lake, some convenient rocks
where two children pose with a father
and the mother is cooking something
in immaculate slacks by a smokeless fire,
her teeth white as detergent.

Whose dream is this, I would like to know:
is this a manufactured
hallucination, a cynical fiction, a lure
for export only?

I seem to remember people,
at least in the cities, also slush,
machines and assorted garbage. Perhaps
that was my private mirage

which will just evaporate
when I go back. Or the citizens will be gone,
run off to the peculiarly-
green forests
to wait among the brownish mountains
for the platoons of tourists
and plan their odd red massacres.

Unsuspecting
window lady, I ask you:

Do you see nothing
watching you from under the water?

Was the sky ever that blue?

Who really lives there?

ELEGY FOR THE GIANT TORTOISES

Let others pray for the passenger pigeon
the dodo, the whooping crane, the eskimo:
everyone must specialize

I will confine myself to a meditation
upon the giant tortoises
withering finally on a remote island.

I concentrate in subway stations,
in parks, I can't quite see them,
they move to the peripheries of my eyes

but on the last day they will be there;
already the event
like a wave travelling shapes vision:

on the road where I stand they will materialize,
plodding past me in a straggling line
awkward without water

their small heads pondering
from side to side, their useless armour
sadder than tanks and history,

in their closed gaze ocean and sunlight paralysed,
lumbering up the steps, under the archways
toward the square glass altars

where the brittle gods are kept,
the relics of what we have destroyed,
our holy and obsolete symbols.

ROOMINGHOUSE, WINTER

Catprints, dogprints, marks
of ancient children
have made the paths we follow

to the vestibule, piled
with overshoes, ownerless letters
a wooden sled.

The threadbare treads
on the stairs. The trails
worn by alien feet

in time through the forest snowdrifts
of the corridor to this remnant, this
discarded door

What disturbs me in the bathroom
is the unclaimed toothbrush.

In the room itself, none
of the furniture is mine.

The plates are on the table
to weight it down.

I call you sometimes
To make sure you are still there.

Tomorrow, when you come to dinner
They will tell you I never lived here.

My window is a funnel
for the shapes of chaos

In the backyard, frozen bones, the children's
voices, derelict
objects

Inside, the wall
buckles; the pressure

balanced by this clear
small silence.

We must resist. We must refuse
to disappear

I said, In exile
survival
is the first necessity.

After that (I say this
tentatively)
we might begin

Survive what? you said.

In the weak light you looked
over your shoulder.
You said

Nobody ever survives.

IT IS DANGEROUS TO READ NEWSPAPERS

While I was building neat
castles in the sandbox,
the hasty pits were
filling with bulldozed corpses
and as I walked to the school
washed and combed, my feet
stepping on the cracks in the cement
detonated red bombs.

Now I am grownup
and literate, and I sit in my chair
as quietly as a fuse

and the jungles are flaming, the under-
brush is charged with soldiers,
the names on the difficult
maps go up in smoke.

I am the cause, I am a stockpile of chemical
toys, my body
is a deadly gadget,
I reach out in love, my hands are guns,
my good intentions are completely lethal.

Even my
passive eyes transmute
everything I look at to the pocked
black and white of a war photo,
how
can I stop myself

It is dangerous to read newspapers.

Each time I hit a key
on my electric typewriter,
speaking of peaceful trees

another village explodes.

PROGRESSIVE INSANITIES OF A PIONEER

i

He stood, a point
on a sheet of green paper
proclaiming himself the centre,

with no walls, no borders
anywhere; the sky no height
above him, totally un-
enclosed
and shouted:

Let me out!

ii

He dug the soil in rows,
imposed himself with shovels
He asserted
into the furrows, I
am not random.

The ground
replied with aphorisms:

a tree-sprout, a nameless
weed, words
he couldn't understand.

iii

The house pitched
the plot staked
in the middle of nowhere.

At night the mind
inside, in the middle
of nowhere.

The idea of an animal
patters across the roof.

In the darkness the fields
defend themselves with fences
in vain:
            everything
            is getting in.

iv

By daylight he resisted.
He said, disgusted
with the swamp's clamourings and the outbursts
of rocks.
            This is not order
            but the absence
            of order.

He was wrong, the unanswering
forest implied:

            It was
            an ordered absence

v

For many years
he fished for a great vision,
dangling the hooks of sown
roots under the surface
of the shallow earth.

It was like
enticing whales with a bent
pin. Besides he thought

in that country
only the worms were biting.

vi

If he had known unstructured
space is a deluge
and stocked his log house-
boat with all the animals

even the wolves,

he might have floated.

But obstinate he
stated, The land is solid
and stamped,

watching his foot sink
down through stone
up to the knee.

vii

Things
refused to name themselves; refused
to let him name them.

The wolves hunted
outside.

On his beaches, his clearings,
by the surf of under-
growth breaking
at his feet, he foresaw
disintegration
                    and in the end
through eyes
made ragged by his
effort, the tension
between subject and object,

the green
vision, the unnamed
whale invaded.

SPEECHES FOR DR FRANKENSTEIN

i

I, the performer
in the tense arena, glittered
under the fluorescent moon. Was bent
masked by the table. Saw what focused
my intent: the emptiness

The air filled with an ether of cheers.

My wrist extended a scalpel.

ii

The table is a flat void,
barren as total freedom. Though behold

A sharp twist
like taking a jar top off

and it is a living
skeleton, mine, round,
that lies on the plate before me

red as a pomegranate,
every cell a hot light.

iii

I circle, confront
my opponent. The thing
refuses to be shaped, it moves
like yeast. I thrust,

the thing fights back.
It dissolves, growls, grows crude claws;

The air is dusty with blood.

It springs. I cut
with delicate precision.

The specimens
ranged on the shelves, applaud.

The thing falls Thud. A cat
anatomized.

O secret
form of the heart, now I have you.

iv

Now I shall ornament you.
What would you like?

Baroque scrolls on your ankles?
A silver navel ?

I am the universal weaver;
I have eight fingers.

I complicate you;
I surround you with intricate ropes.

What web shall I wrap you in?
Gradually I pin you down.

What equation shall
I carve and seal in your skull?

What size will I make you?
Where should I put your eyes?

v

I was insane with skill:
I made you perfect.

I should have chosen instead
to curl you small as a seed,

trusted beginnings. Now I wince
before this plateful of results:

core and rind, the flesh between
already turning rotten.

I stand in the presence
of the destroyed god:

a rubble of tendons,
knuckles and raw sinews.

Knowing that the work is mine
how can I love you?

These archives of potential
time exude fear like a smell.

vi

You arise, larval
and shrouded in the flesh I gave you;

I, who have no covering
left but a white cloth skin

escape from you. You are red,
you are human and distorted.

You have been starved,
you are hungry. I have nothing to feed you.

I pull around me, running,
a cape of rain.

What was my ravenous motive?
Why did I make you?

vii

Reflection, you have stolen
everything you needed:

my joy, my ability
to suffer.

You have transmuted
yourself to me: I am
a vestige, I am numb.

Now you accuse me of murder.

Can't you see
I am incapable?

Blood of my brain,
it is you who have killed these people.

viii

Since I dared
to attempt impious wonders

I must pursue
that animal I once denied
was mine.

Over this vacant winter
plain, the sky is a black shell;
I move within it, a cold
kernel of pain.

I scratch huge rescue messages
on the solid
snow; in vain. My heart's
husk is a stomach. I am its food.

ix

The sparkling monster
gambols there ahead,
his mane electric:
This is his true place.

He dances in spirals on the ice,
his clawed feet
kindling shaggy fires.

His happiness
is now the chase itself:
he traces it in light,
his paths contain it.

I am the gaunt hunter
necessary for his patterns,
lurking, gnawing leather.

x

The creature, his arctic hackles
bristling, spreads
over the dark ceiling,
his paws on the horizons,
rolling the world like a snowball.

He glows and says:

Doctor, my shadow
shivering on the table,
you dangle on the leash
of your own longing;
your need grows teeth.

You sliced me loose

and said it was
Creation. I could feel the knife.
Now you would like to heal
that chasm in your side,
but I recede. I prowl.

I will not come when you call.

BACKDROP ADDRESSES COWBOY

Starspangled cowboy
sauntering out of the almost-
silly West, on your face
a porcelain grin,
tugging a papier-mâché cactus
on wheels behind you with a string,

you are innocent as a bathtub
full of bullets.

Your righteous eyes, your laconic
trigger-fingers
people the streets with villains:
as you move, the air in front of you
blossoms with targets

and you leave behind you a heroic
trail of desolation:
beer bottles
slaughtered by the side
of the road, bird-
skulls bleaching in the sunset.

I ought to be watching
from behind a cliff or a cardboard storefront
when the shooting starts, hands clasped
in admiration,

but I am elsewhere.

Then what about me

what about the I
confronting you on that border
you are always trying to cross?

I am the horizon
you ride towards, the thing you can never lasso

I am also what surrounds you:
my brain
scattered with your
tincans, bones, empty shells,
the litter of your invasions.

I am the space you desecrate
as you pass through.

I WAS READING A SCIENTIFIC ARTICLE

They have photographed the brain
and here is the picture, it is full of
branches as I always suspected,

each time you arrive the electricity
of seeing you is a huge
tree lumbering through my skull, the roots waving.

It is an earth, its fibres wrap
things buried, your forgotten words
are graved in my head, an intricate

red blue and pink prehensile chemistry
veined like a leaf
network, or is it a seascape
with corals and shining tentacles.

I touch you, I am created in you
somewhere as a complex
filament of light

You rest on me and my shoulder holds

your heavy unbelievable
skull, crowded with radiant
suns, a new planet, the people
submerged in you, a lost civilization
I can never excavate:

my hands trace the contours of a total
universe, its different
colours, flowers, its undiscovered
animals, violent or serene

its other air
its claws

its paradise rivers

MORE AND MORE

More and more frequently the edges
of me dissolve and I become
a wish to assimilate the world, including
you, if possible through the skin
like a cool plant's tricks with oxygen
and live by a harmless green burning.

I would not consume
you, or ever
finish, you would still be there
surrounding me, complete
as the air.

Unfortunately I don't have leaves.
Instead I have eyes
and teeth and other non-green
things which rule out osmosis.

So be careful, I mean it,
I give you a fair warning:

This kind of hunger draws
everything into its own
space; nor can we
talk it all over, have a calm
rational discussion.

There is no reason for this, only
a starved dog's logic about bones.

A VOICE

A voice from the other country
stood on the grass. He became
part of the grass.

        The sun shone
        greenly on the blades of his hands

Then we
appeared, climbing down
the hill, you
in your blue sweater.

He could see that
we did not occupy
the space, as he did. We
were merely in it

        My skirt was yellow
        small
        between his eyes

We moved along
            the grass, through
the air that was inside
his head. We did not see him.

            He could smell
            the leather on our feet

We walked
small
across
his field of vision (he
watching us) and disappeared.

            His brain grew over
            the places we had been.

He sat. He was curious
about himself. He wondered
how he had managed to think us.

THE REINCARNATION OF CAPTAIN COOK

Earlier than I could learn
the maps had been coloured in.
When I pleaded, the kings told me
nothing was left to explore.

I set out anyway, but
everywhere I went
there were historians, wearing
wreaths and fake teeth
belts; or in the deserts, cairns
and tourists. Even the caves had
candle stubs, inscriptions quickly
scribbled in darkness. I could

never arrive. Always
the names got there before.

Now I am old I know my
mistake was my acknowledging
of maps. The eyes raise
tired monuments.

Burn down
the atlases, I shout
to the park benches; and go

past the cenotaph
waving a blank banner
across the street, beyond
the corner

into a new land cleaned of geographies,
its beach gleaming with arrows.

AXIOM

Axiom: you are a sea.
Your eye-
lids curve over chaos

My hands
where they touch you, create
small inhabited islands

Soon you will be
all earth: a known
land, a country.

The Journals of Susanna Moodie

1970

DISEMBARKING AT QUEBEC

Is it my clothes, my way of walking,
the things I carry in my hand
– a book, a bag with knitting –
the incongruous pink of my shawl

this space cannot hear

or is it my own lack
of conviction which makes
these vistas of desolation,
long hills, the swamps, the barren sand, the glare
of sun on the bone-white
driftlogs, omens of winter,
the moon alien in day-
time a thin refusal

The others leap, shout

Freedom!

The moving water will not show me
my reflection.

The rocks ignore.

I am a word
in a foreign language.

FURTHER ARRIVALS

After we had crossed the long illness
that was the ocean, we sailed up-river

On the first island
the immigrants threw off their clothes
and danced like sandflies

We left behind one by one
the cities rotting with cholera,
one by one our civilized
distinctions

and entered a large darkness.

It was our own
ignorance we entered.

I have not come out yet

My brain gropes nervous
tentacles in the night, sends out
fears hairy as bears,
demands lamps; or waiting

for my shadowy husband, hears
malice in the trees' whispers.

I need wolf's eyes to see
the truth.

I refuse to look in a mirror.

Whether the wilderness is
real or not
depends on who lives there.

FIRST NEIGHBOURS

The people I live among, unforgivingly
previous to me, grudging
the way I breathe their
property, the air,
speaking a twisted dialect to my differently-
shaped ears

though I tried to adapt

(the girl in a red tattered
petticoat, who jeered at me for my burned bread

Go back where you came from

I tightened my lips; knew that England
was now unreachable, had sunk down into the sea
without ever teaching me about washtubs)

got used to being
a minor invalid, expected to make
inept remarks,
futile and spastic gestures

(asked the Indian
about the squat thing on a stick
drying by the fire: Is that a toad?
Annoyed, he said No no,
deer liver, very good)

Finally I grew a chapped tarpaulin
skin; I negotiated the drizzle
of strange meaning, set it
down to just the latitude:
something to be endured
but not surprised by.

Inaccurate. The forest can still trick me:
one afternoon while I was drawing
birds, a malignant face
flickered over my shoulder;
the branches quivered.

Resolve: to be both tentative and hard to startle
(though clumsiness and
fright are inevitable)

in this area where my damaged
knowing of the language means
prediction is forever impossible

THE PLANTERS

They move between the jagged edge
of the forest and the jagged river
on a stumpy patch of cleared land

my husband, a neighbour, another man
weeding the few rows
of string beans and dusty potatoes.

They bend, straighten; the sun
lights up their faces and hands, candles
flickering in the wind against the

unbright earth. I see them; I know
none of them believe they are here.
They deny the ground they stand on,

pretend this dirt is the future.
And they are right. If they let go
of that illusion solid to them as a shovel,

open their eyes even for a moment
to these trees, to this particular sun
they would be surrounded, stormed, broken

in upon by branches, roots, tendrils, the dark
side of light
as I am.

THE WEREMAN

My husband walks in the frosted field
an X, a concept
defined against a blank;
he swerves, enters the forest
and is blotted out.

Unheld by my sight
what does he change into
what other shape
blends with the under-
growth, wavers across the pools
is camouflaged from the listening
swamp animals

At noon he will
return; or it may be
only my idea of him
I will find returning
with him hiding behind it.

He may change me also
with the fox eye, the owl
eye, the eightfold
eye of the spider

I can't think
what he will see
when he opens the door

PATHS AND THINGSCAPE

Those who went ahead
of us in the forest
bent the early trees
so that they grew to signals:

the trail was not
among the trees but
the trees

and there are some who have dreams
of birds flying in the shapes
of letters; the sky's
codes;
        and dream also
the significance of numbers (count
petals of certain flowers)

    In the morning I advance
    through the doorway: the sun
    on the bark, the inter-
    twisted branches, here
    a blue movement in the leaves, dispersed
    calls/ no trails; rocks
    and grey tufts of moss

    The petals of the fire-
    weed fall where they fall

I am watched like an invader
who knows hostility but
not where

The day shrinks back from me

When will be
that union and each
thing (bits
of surface broken by my foot
step) will without moving move
around me
into its place

THE TWO FIRES

One, the summer fire
outside: the trees melting, returning
to their first red elements
on all sides, cutting me off
from escape or the saving
lake

I sat in the house, raised up
between that shapeless raging
and my sleeping children
a charm: concentrate on
form, geometry, the human
architecture of the house, square
closed doors, proved roofbeams,
the logic of windows

(the children could not be wakened:
in their calm dreaming
the trees were straight and still
had branches and were green)

The other, the winter
fire inside: the protective roof
shrivelling overhead, the rafters
incandescent, all those corners
and straight lines flaming, the carefully-
made structure
prisoning us in a cage of blazing
bars
      the children
were awake and crying;

I wrapped them, carried them
outside into the snow.
Then I tried to rescue
what was left of their scorched dream
about the house: blankets,
warm clothes, the singed furniture
of safety cast away with them
in a white chaos

Two fires in-
formed me,

(each refuge fails
us; each danger
becomes a haven)

left charred marks
now around which I
try to grow

LOOKING IN A MIRROR

It was as if I woke
after a sleep of seven years

to find stiff lace, religious
black rotted
off by earth and the strong waters

and instead my skin thickened
with bark and the white hairs of roots

My heirloom face I brought
with me a crushed eggshell
among other debris:
the china plate shattered
on the forest road, the shawl
from India decayed, pieces of letters

and the sun here had stained
me its barbarous colour

Hands grown stiff, the fingers
brittle as twigs
eyes bewildered after
seven years, and almost
blind/ buds, which can see
only the wind

the mouth cracking
open like a rock in fire
trying to say

What is this

(you find only
the shape you already are
but what
if you have forgotten that
or discover you
have never known)

DEPARTURE FROM THE BUSH

I, who had been erased
by fire, was crept in
upon by green
                    (how
lucid a season)

                    In time the animals
arrived to inhabit me,

first one
   by one, stealthily
(their habitual traces
burnt); then
having marked new boundaries
returning, more
confident, year
by year, two
by two

but restless: I was not ready
altogether to be moved into

They could tell I was
too heavy: I might
capsize;

I was frightened
by their eyes (green or
amber) glowing out from inside me

I was not completed; at night
I could not see without lanterns.

He wrote, We are leaving. I said
I have no clothes
left I can wear

The snow came. The sleigh was a relief;
its track lengthened behind,
pushing me towards the city

and rounding the first hill, I was
(instantaneous)
unlived in: they had gone.

There was something they almost taught me
I came away not having learned.

DEATH OF A YOUNG SON BY DROWNING

He, who navigated with success
the dangerous river of his own birth
once more set forth

on a voyage of discovery
into the land I floated on
but could not touch to claim.

His feet slid on the bank,
the currents took him;
he swirled with ice and trees in the swollen water

and plunged into distant regions,
his head a bathysphere;
through his eyes' thin glass bubbles

he looked out, reckless adventurer
on a landscape stranger than Uranus
we have all been to and some remember.

There was an accident; the air locked,
he was hung in the river like a heart.
They retrieved the swamped body,

cairn of my plans and future charts,
with poles and hooks
from among the nudging logs.

It was spring, the sun kept shining, the new grass
leapt to solidity;
my hands glistened with details.

After the long trip I was tired of waves.
My foot hit rock. The dreamed sails
collapsed, ragged.

I planted him in this country
like a flag.

THE IMMIGRANTS

They are allowed to inherit
the sidewalks involved as palmlines, bricks
exhausted and soft, the deep
lawnsmells, orchards whorled
to the land's contours, the inflected weather

only to be told they are too poor
to keep it up, or someone
has noticed and wants to kill them; or the towns
pass laws which declare them obsolete.

I see them coming
up from the hold smelling of vomit,
infested, emaciated, their skins grey
with travel; as they step on shore

the old countries recede, become
perfect, thumbnail castles preserved
like gallstones in a glass bottle, the
towns dwindle upon the hillsides
in a light paperweight-clear.

They carry their carpetbags and trunks
with clothes, dishes, the family pictures;
they think they will make an order
like the old one, sow miniature orchards,
carve children and flocks out of wood

but always they are too poor, the sky
is flat, the green fruit shrivels
in the prairie sun, wood is for burning;
and if they go back, the towns

in time have crumbled, their tongues
stumble among awkward teeth, their ears
are filled with the sound of breaking glass.
I wish I could forget them
and so forget myself:

my mind is a wide pink map
across which move year after year
arrows and dotted lines, further and further,
people in railway cars

their heads stuck out of the windows
at stations, drinking milk or singing,
their features hidden with beards or shawls
day and night riding across an ocean of unknown
land to an unknown land.

DREAM 1: THE BUSH GARDEN

I stood once more in that garden
sold, deserted and
gone to seed

In the dream I could
see down through the earth, could see
the potatoes curled
like pale grubs in the soil
the radishes thrusting down
their fleshy snouts, the beets
pulsing like slow amphibian hearts

Around my feet
the strawberries were surging, huge
and shining

When I bent
to pick, my hands
came away red and wet

In the dream I said
I should have known
anything planted here
would come up blood

1837 WAR IN RETROSPECT

One of the
things I found out by being
there, and after:

that history (that list
of ballooning wishes, flukes,
bent times, plunges and mistakes
clutched like parachutes)

is rolling itself up in your head
at one end and unrolling at the other

that this war will soon be among
those tiny ancestral figures
flickering dull white through the back of your skull,
confused, anxious, not sure any more
what they are doing there

appearing from time to time
with idiot faces and hands clusters
of bananas, holding flags,
holding guns, advancing through the trees
brown line green scribble

or crouching within a rough grey
crayon diagram of a fort,
shooting at each other, the smoke and red fire
made actual through a child's fingers.

DREAM 2: BRIAN THE STILL-HUNTER

The man I saw in the forest
used to come to our house
every morning, never said anything;
I learned from the neighbours later
he once tried to cut his throat.

I found him at the end of the path
sitting on a fallen tree
cleaning his gun.

There was no wind;
around us the leaves rustled.

He said to me:
I kill because I have to

but every time I aim, I feel
my skin grow fur
my head heavy with antlers
and during the stretched instant
the bullet glides on its thread of speed
my soul runs innocent as hooves.

Is God just to his creatures?

I die more often than many.

He looked up and I saw
the white scar made by the hunting knife
around his neck.

When I woke
I remembered: he has been gone
twenty years and not heard from.

CHARIVARI

'They capped their heads with feathers, masked
their faces, wore their clothes backwards, howled
with torches through the midnight winter

and dragged the black man from his house
to the jolting music of broken
instruments, pretending to each other

it was a joke, until
they killed him. I don't know
what happened to the white bride.'

The American lady, adding she
thought it was a disgraceful piece
of business, finished her tea.

(Note: Never pretend this isn't
part of the soil too, teadrinkers, and inadvertent
victims and murderers, when we come this way

again in other forms, take care
to look behind, within
where the skeleton face beneath

the face puts on its feather mask, the arm
within the arm lifts up the spear:
Resist those cracked

drumbeats. Stop this. Become human.)

DREAM 3: NIGHT BEAR WHICH FRIGHTENED CATTLE

Horns crowding toward us
a stampede of bellowing, one
night the surface of my mind keeps
only as anecdote

We laughed, safe with lanterns
at the kitchen door

though beneath stories

where forgotten birds
tremble through memory, ripples across water
and a moon hovers in the lake
orange and prehistoric

I lean with my feet grown intangible
because I am not there

watching the bear I didn't see condense
itself among the trees, an outline
tenuous as an echo

but it is real, heavier
than real   I know
even by daylight here
in this visible kitchen

it absorbs all terror

it moves toward the lighted cabin
below us on the slope
where my family gathers

a mute vibration passing
between my ears

THE DEATHS OF THE OTHER CHILDREN

The body dies

little by little

the body buries itself

joins itself
to the loosened mind, to the black-
berries and thistles, running in a
thorny wind
over the shallow
fountations of our former houses,
dim hollows now in the sandy soil

Did I spend all those years
building up this edifice
my composite
                    self, this crumbling hovel?

My arms, my eyes, my grieving
words, my disintegrated children

Everywhere I walk, along
the overgrowing paths, my skirt
tugged at by the spreading briers

they catch at my heels with their fingers

THE DOUBLE VOICE

Two voices
took turns using my eyes:

One had manners,
painted in watercolours,
used hushed tones when speaking
of mountains or Niagara Falls,
composed uplifting verse
and expended sentiment upon the poor.

The other voice
had other knowledge:
that men sweat
always and drink often,
that pigs are pigs
but must be eaten
anyway, that unborn babies
fester like wounds in the body,
that there is nothing to be done
about mosquitoes;

One saw through my
bleared and gradually
bleaching eyes, red leaves,
the rituals of seasons and rivers

The other found a dead dog
jubilant with maggots
half-buried among the sweet peas.

LATER IN BELLEVILLE: CAREER

Once by a bitter candle
of oil and braided
rags, I wrote
verses about love and sleighbells

which I exchanged for potatoes;

in the summers I painted butterflies
on a species of white fungus
which were bought by the tourists, glass-
cased for English parlours

and my children (miraculous)
wore shoes.

Now every day
I sit on a stuffed sofa
in my own fringed parlour, have
uncracked plates (from which I eat
at intervals)
and a china teaset.

There is no use for art.

DAGUERREOTYPE TAKEN IN OLD AGE

I know I change
have changed

but whose is this vapid face
pitted and vast, rotund
suspended in empty paper
as though in a telescope

the granular moon

I rise from my chair
pulling against gravity
I turn away
and go out into the garden

I revolve among the vegetables,
my head ponderous
reflecting the sun
in shadows from the pocked ravines
cut in my cheeks, my eye-
sockets 2 craters

along the paths
I orbit
the apple trees
white white spinning
stars around me

I am being
eaten away by light

WISH: METAMORPHOSIS TO HERALDIC EMBLEM

I balance myself carefully
inside my shrinking body
which is nevertheless
deceptive as a cat's fur:

when I am dipped in the earth
I will be much smaller.

On my skin the wrinkles branch
out, overlapping like hair or feathers.

In this parlour my grandchildren
uneasy on sunday chairs
with my deafness, my cameo brooch
my puckered mind
scurrying in its old burrows

little guess how
                        maybe

I will prowl and slink
in crystal darkness
among the stalactite roots, with new
formed plumage
                        uncorroded
                                              gold and

Fiery green, my fingers
curving and scaled, my

opal
        no
    eyes glowing

VISIT TO TORONTO, WITH COMPANIONS

The streets are new, the harbour
is new also;
the lunatic asylum is yellow.

On the first floor there were
women sitting, sewing;
they looked at us sadly, gently,
answered questions.

On the second floor there were
women crouching, thrashing,
tearing off their clothes, screaming;
to us they paid little attention.

On the third floor
I went through a glass-panelled
door into a different kind of room.
It was a hill, with boulders, trees, no houses.
I sat down and smoothed my gloves.

The landscape was saying something
but I couldn't hear. One of the rocks
sighed and rolled over.

Above me, at eye level
three faces appeared in an oblong space.

They wanted me to go out
to where there were streets and
the Toronto harbour

I shook my head. There were no clouds, the flowers
deep red and feathered, shot from among
the dry stones,
                                        the air
was about to tell me
all kinds of answers

SOLIPSISM WHILE DYING

the skeleton produces flesh   enemy
opposing, then taken
for granted, earth harvested, used
up, walked over

the ears produce sounds   what I heard I
created. (voices
determining, repeating
histories, worn customs

the mouth produces words   I said I created
myself, and these
frames, commas, calendars
that enclose me

the hands produce objects   the world touched
into existence: was
this cup, this village here
before my fingers

the eyes produce light   the sky
leaps at me: let there be
the sun-
set

Or so I thought, lying in the bed
being regretted

added: What will they do now
that I, that all
depending on me disappears?

Where will be Belleville?

Kingston?

(the fields
I held between. the lake
boats

t o r o N T O

THOUGHTS FROM UNDERGROUND

When I first reached this country
I hated it
and I hated it more each year:

in summer the light a
violent blur, the heat
thick as a swamp,
the green things fiercely
shoving themselves upwards, the
eyelids bitten by insects

In winter our teeth were brittle
with cold. We fed on squirrels.
At night the house cracked.
In the mornings, we thawed
the bad bread over the stove.

Then we were made successful
and I felt I ought to love
this country.
I said I loved it
and my mind saw double.

I began to forget myself
in the middle
of sentences. Events
were split apart

I fought. I constructed
desperate paragraphs of praise, everyone
ought to love it because

and set them up at intervals

        due to natural resources, native industry, superior
        penitentiaries
        we will all be rich and powerful
  flat as highway billboards

          who can doubt it, look how
          fast Belleville is growing

  (though it is still no place for an english gentleman)

ALTERNATE THOUGHTS FROM UNDERGROUND

Down. Shovelled. Can hear
faintly laughter, footsteps;
the shrill of glass and steel

the invaders of those for whom
shelter was wood,
fire was terror and sacred

the inheritors, the raisers
of glib superstructures.

My heart silted by decades
of older thoughts, yet prays

O topple this glass pride, fireless
rivetted babylon, prays
through subsoil
to my wooden fossil God.

But they prevail. Extinct. I feel
scorn but also pity: what
the bones of the giant reptiles

done under by the thing
(may call it
climate) outside the circle
they drew by their closed senses
of what was right

felt when scuttled
across, nested in by the velvet immoral
uncalloused and armourless mammals.

RESURRECTION

I see now I see
now I cannot see

earth is a blizzard in my eyes

I hear now

the rustle of the snow

the angels listening above me

thistles bright with sleet
gathering

waiting for the time
to reach me
up to the pillared
sun, the final city

or living towers

unrisen yet
whose dormant stones lie folding
their holy fire around me

(but the land shifts with frost
and those who have become the stone
voices of the land
shift also and say

god is not
the voice in the whirlwind

god is the whirlwind

at the last
judgement we will all be trees

A BUS ALONG ST CLAIR: DECEMBER

It would take more than that to banish
me: this is my kingdom still.

Turn, look up
through the gritty window: an unexplored
wilderness of wires

Though they buried me in monuments
of concrete slabs, of cables
though they mounded a pyramid
of cold light over my head
though they said, We will build
silver paradise with a bulldozer

it shows how little they know
about vanishing: I have
my ways of getting through.

Right now, the snow
is no more familiar
to you than it was to me:
this is my doing.
The grey air, the roar
going on behind it
are no more familiar.

I am the old woman
sitting across from you on the bus,
her shoulders drawn up like a shawl;
out of her eyes come secret
hatpins, destroying
the walls, the ceiling

Turn, look down:
there is no city;
this is the centre of a forest

your place is empty

From

Procedures for Underground

1970

GAME AFTER SUPPER

This is before electricity,
it is when there were porches.

On the sagging porch an old man
is rocking. The porch is wooden,

the house is wooden and grey;
in the living room which smells of
smoke and mildew, soon
the woman will light the kerosene lamp.

There is a barn but I am not in the barn;
there is an orchard too, gone bad,
its apples like soft cork
but I am not there either.

I am hiding in the long grass
with my two dead cousins,
the membrane grown already
across their throats.

We hear crickets and our own hearts
close to our ears;
though we giggle, we are afraid.

From the shadows around
the corner of the house
a tall man is coming to find us:

He will be an uncle,
if we are lucky.

GIRL AND HORSE, 1928

You are younger than I am, you are
someone I never knew, you stand
under a tree, your face half-shadowed,
holding the horse by its bridle.

Why do you smile? Can't you
see the apple blossoms falling around
you, snow, sun, snow, listen, the tree
dries and is being burnt, the wind

is bending your body, your face
ripples like water   where did you go
But no, you stand there exactly
the same, you can't hear me, forty

years ago you were caught by light
and fixed in that secret
place where we live, where we believe
nothing can change, grow older.

(On the other side
of the picture, the instant
is over, the shadow
of the tree has moved. You wave,

then turn and ride
out of sight through the vanished
orchard, still smiling
as though you do not notice)

THE SMALL CABIN

The house we built gradually
from the ground up when we were young
(three rooms, the walls
raw trees) burned down
last year   they said

I didn't see it, and so
the house is still there in me

among branches as always   I stand
inside it looking out
at the rain moving across the lake

but when I go back
to the empty place in the forest
the house will blaze and crumple
suddenly in my mind

collapsing like a cardboard carton
thrown on a bonfire, summers
crackling, my earlier
selves outlined in flame.

Left in my head will be
the blackened earth: the truth.

Where did the house go?

Where do the words go
when we have said them?

PROCEDURES FOR UNDERGROUND
(Northwest Coast)

The country beneath
the earth has a green sun
and the rivers flow backwards;

the trees and rocks are the same
as they are here, but shifted.
Those who live there are always hungry;

from them you can learn
wisdom and great power,
if you can descend and return safely.

You must look for tunnels, animal
burrows or the cave in the sea
guarded by the stone man;

when you are down you will find
those who were once your friends
but they will be changed and dangerous.

Resist them, be careful
never to eat their food.
Afterwards, if you live, you will be able

to see them when they prowl as winds,
as thin sounds in our village. You will
tell us their names, what they want, who

has made them angry by forgetting them.
For this gift, as for all gifts, you must
suffer: those from the underland

will be always with you, whispering their
complaints, beckoning you
back down; while among us here

you will walk wrapped in an invisible
cloak. Few will seek your help
with love, none without fear.

DREAMS OF THE ANIMALS

Mostly the animals dream
of other animals   each
according to its kind

(though certain mice and small rodents
have nightmares of a huge pink
shape with five claws descending)

: moles dream of darkness and delicate
mole smells

frogs dream of green and golden
frogs
sparkling like wet suns
among the lilies

red and black
striped fish, their eyes open
have red and black striped
dreams   defence, attack, meaningful
patterns

birds dream of territories
enclosed by singing.

Sometimes the animals dream of evil
in the form of soap and metal
but mostly the animals dream
of other animals.

There are exceptions:

> the silver fox in the roadside zoo
> dreams of digging out
> and of baby foxes, their necks bitten
>
> the caged armadillo
> near the train
> station, which runs
> all day in figure eights
> its piglet feet pattering,
> no longer dreams
> but is insane when waking;
>
> the iguana
> in the petshop window on St Catherine Street
> crested, royal-eyed, ruling
> its kingdom of water-dish and sawdust
>
> dreams of sawdust.

CYCLOPS

You, going along the path,
mosquito-doped, with no moon, the flashlight
a single orange eye

unable to see what is beyond
the capsule of your dim
sight, what shape

contracts to a heart
with terror, bumps
among the leaves, what makes
a bristling noise like a fur throat

Is it true you do not wish to hurt them?

Is it true you have no fear?
Take off your shoes then,
let your eyes go bare,
swim in their darkness as in a river

do not disguise
yourself in armour.

They watch you from hiding:
you are a chemical
smell, a cold fire, you are
giant and indefinable

In their monstrous night
thick with possible claws
where danger is not knowing,

you are the hugest monster.

THREE DESK OBJECTS

What suns had to rise and set
what eyes had to blink out
what hands and fingers
had to let go of their heat

before you appeared on my desk
black light
portable and radiant

and you, my electric typewriter
with your cord and hungry plug
drinking a sinister transfusion
from the other side of the wall

what histories of slaughter
have left these scars on your keys

What multiple deaths have set loose this clock
the small wheels that grind
their teeth under the metal scalp

My cool machines
resting there so familiar
so hard and perfect

I am afraid to touch you
I think you will cry out in pain

I think you will be warm, like skin.

PROJECTED SLIDE OF AN UNKNOWN SOLDIER

Upon the wall a face
uttered itself
in light, pushing
aside the wall's darkness;

Around it leaves, glossy,
perhaps tropical, not making
explicit whether the face was
breaking through them, wore them

as disguise, was crowned
with them or sent them
forth as rays,
a slippery halo;

The clothes were invisible,
the eyes
hidden; the nose
foreshortened: a muzzle.
Hair on the upper lip.
On the skin the light shone, wet
with heat; the teeth
of the open mouth reflected it
as absolute.

The mouth was open
stretched wide in a call or howl
(there was no tongue)
of agony, ultimate
command or simple famine.
The canine teeth ranged back
into the throat and vanished.

The mouth was filled with darkness.
The darkness in the open mouth
uttered itself, pushing
aside the light.

COMIC BOOKS VS. HISTORY (1949, 1969)

On the blackboard map your country
was erased, blank, waiting
to be filled with whatever shapes
we chose:

tense
needle turrets of steel
cities

heroes
lived there, we knew

they all wore capes, bullets
bounced off them;
from their fists came beautiful
orange collisions.

Our side was coloured in
with dots and letters
but it held only
real-sized explorers, confined
to animal skin coats;

they plodded, discovered
rivers whose names we always
forgot; in the winters
they died of scurvy.

When I reached that other
shore finally, statistics
and diseased labels multiplied
everywhere in my head

space contracted, the
red and silver
heroes had collapsed inside
their rubber suits / the riddled
buildings were decaying
magic

I turn back, search
for the actual, collect lost
bones, burnt logs
of campfires, pieces of fur.

WOMAN SKATING

A lake sunken among
cedar and black spruce hills;
late afternoon.

On the ice a woman skating,
jacket sudden
red against the white,

concentrating on moving
in perfect circles.

> (actually she is my mother, she is
> over at the outdoor skating rink
> near the cemetery. On three sides
> of her there are streets of brown
> brick houses; cars go by; on the
> fourth side is the park building.
> The snow banked around the rink
> is grey with soot. She never skates
> here. She's wearing a sweater and
> faded maroon earmuffs, she has
> taken off her gloves)

Now near the horizon
the enlarged pink sun swings down.
Soon it will be zero.

With arms wide the skater
turns, leaving her breath like a diver's
trail of bubbles.

Seeing the ice
as what it is, water:
seeing the months

as they are, the years
in sequence occurring
underfoot, watching
the miniature human
figure balanced on steel
needles (those compasses
floated in saucers) on time
sustained, above
time circling: miracle

Over all I place
a glass bell

YOUNGER SISTER, GOING SWIMMING
(Northern Quebec)

Beside this lake
where there are no other people

my sister in bathing suit continues
her short desolate
parade to the end of the dock;

against the boards
her feet make sad statements
she thinks no one can hear;

(I sit in a deckchair
not counting, invisible;
the sun wavers on
this page as on a pool.)

She moves the raft out
past the sandy point;
no one comes by in a motorboat.

She would like to fill the lake
with other swimmers, with answers.
She calls her name. The sun encloses
rocks, trees, her feet in the water, the circling
bays and hills as before.

She poises, raises her arms
as though signalling, then disappears.
The lake heals itself quietly
of the wound left by the diver.
The air quakes and is still.

(Under my hand the paper
closes over these
marks I am making on it.

The words ripple, subside,
move outwards toward the shore.)

FISHING FOR EEL TOTEMS

I stood on the reed bank
ear tuned to the line, listening
to the signals from the ones who lived
under the blue barrier,

thinking they had no words for things
in the air.

The string jumped,
I hooked a martian / it poured
fluid silver out of the river

its long body whipped on the grass, reciting
all the letters of its alphabet.

Killed, it was a
grey tongue hanged silent in the smokehouse

which we later ate.

After that I could see
for a time in the green country;

I learned that the earliest language
was not our syntax of chained pebbles

but liquid, made
by the first tribes, the fish
people.

BUFFALO IN COMPOUND: ALBERTA

The marsh flat where they graze
beside the stream is
late afternoon, serene
with slanted light: green leaves are
yellow: even
the mud shines

Placid, they bend down
silently to the grass;
when they move, the small birds
follow, settle almost
under their feet.

Fenced out but anxious
anyway, and glad our car is
near, we press
close to the wire
squares, our hands raised
for shields
against the sun, which is
everywhere

It was hard to see them
but we thought we saw
in the field near them, the god
of this place: brutal,
zeus-faced, his horned
head man-bearded, his
fused red eye turned inward
to cloudburst and pounded earth, the water-
falling of hooves fisted inside
a calm we would call madness.

Then they were going
in profile, one by one, their
firelit outlines fixed as carvings

backs to us now
they enter
the shade of the gold-edged trees

CARRYING FOOD HOME IN WINTER

I walk uphill through the snow
hard going
brown paper bag of groceries
balanced low on my stomach,
heavy, my arms stretching
to hold it turn all tendon.

Do we need this paper bag
my love, do we need this bulk
of peels and cores, do we need
these bottles, these roots
and bits of cardboard
to keep us floating
as on a raft
above the snow I sink through?

The skin creates
islands of warmth
in winter, in summer
islands of coolness.

The mouth performs
a similar deception.

I say I will transform
this egg into a muscle
this bottle into an act of love

This onion will become a motion
this grapefruit
will become a thought.

From

Power Politics

1971

you fit into me
like a hook into an eye

a fish hook
an open eye

You take my hand and
I'm suddenly in a bad movie,
it goes on and on and
why am I fascinated

We waltz in slow motion
through an air stale with aphorisms
we meet behind endless potted palms
you climb through the wrong windows

Other people are leaving
but I always stay till the end
I paid my money, I
want to see what happens.

In chance bathtubs I have to
peel you off me
in the form of smoke and melted
celluloid

                Have to face it I'm
finally an addict,
the smell of popcorn and worn plush
lingers for weeks

SHE CONSIDERS EVADING HIM

I can change my-
self more easily
than I can change you

I could grow bark and
become a shrub

or switch back in time
to the woman image left
in cave rubble, the drowned
stomach bulbed with fertility,
face a tiny bead, a
lump, queen of the termites

or (better) speed myself up,
disguise myself in the knuckles
and purple-veined veils of old ladies,
become arthritic and genteel

or one twist further:
collapse across your
bed clutching my heart
and pull the nostalgic sheet up over
my waxed farewell smile

which would be inconvenient
but final.

THEY EAT OUT

In restaurants we argue
over which of us will pay for your funeral

though the real question is
whether or not I will make you immortal.

At the moment only I
can do it and so

I raise the magic fork
over the plate of beef fried rice

and plunge it into your heart.
There is a faint pop, a sizzle

and through your own split head
you rise up glowing;

the ceiling opens
a voice sings Love Is A Many

Splendoured Thing
you hang suspended above the city

in blue tights and a red cape,
your eyes flashing in unison.

The other diners regard you
some with awe, some only with boredom:

they cannot decide if you are a new weapon
or only a new advertisement.

As for me, I continue eating;
I liked you better the way you were,
but you were always ambitious.

After the agony in the guest
bedroom, you lying by the
overturned bed
your face uplifted, neck propped
against the windowsill, my arm
under you, cold moon
shining down through the window

wine mist rising
around you, an almost-
visible halo

You say, Do you
love me, do you love me

I answer you:
I stretch your arms out
one to either side,
your head slumps forward.

Later I take you home
in a taxi, and you
are sick in the bathtub

My beautiful wooden leader
with your heartful of medals
made of wood, fixing it
each time so you almost win,

you long to be bandaged
before you have been cut.
My love for you is the love
of one statue for another: tensed

and static. General, you enlist
my body in your heroic
struggle to become real:
though you promise bronze rescues

you hold me by the left ankle
so that my head brushes the ground,
my eyes are blinded,
my hair fills with white ribbons.

There are hordes of me now, alike
and paralysed, we follow you
scattering floral tributes
under your hooves.

Magnificent on your wooden horse
you point with your fringed hand;
the sun sets, and the people all
ride off in the other direction.

You want to go back
to where the sky was inside us

animals ran through us, our hands
blessed and killed according to our
wisdom, death
made real blood come out

But face it, we have been
improved, our heads float
several inches above our necks
moored to us by
rubber tubes and filled with
clever bubbles,

                    our bodies
are populated with billions
of soft pink numbers
multiplying and analyzing
themselves, perfecting
their own demands, no trouble to anyone.

I love you by
sections and when you work.

Do you want to be illiterate?
This is the way it is, get used to it.

THEIR ATTITUDES DIFFER

i

To understand
each other: anything
but that, & to avoid it

I will suspend my search for
germs if you will keep
your fingers off the microfilm
hidden inside my skin

ii

I approach this love
like a biologist
pulling on my rubber
gloves & white labcoat

You flee from it
like an escaped political
prisoner, and no wonder

iii

You held out your hand
I took your fingerprints

You asked for love
I gave you only descriptions

Please die I said
so I can write about it

After all you are quite
ordinary: 2 arms 2 legs
a head, a reasonable
body, toes & fingers, a few
eccentricities, a few honesties
but not too many, too many
postponements & regrets but

you'll adjust to it, meeting
deadlines and other
people, pretending to love
the wrong woman some of the
time, listening to your brain
shrink, your diaries
expanding as you grow older,

growing older, of course you'll
die but not yet, you'll outlive
even my distortions of you

and there isn't anything
I want to do about the fact
that you are unhappy & sick

you aren't sick & unhappy
only alive & stuck with it.

yes at first you
go down smooth as
pills, all of me
breathes you in and then it's

a kick in the head, orange
and brutal, sharp jewels
hit and my
hair splinters

                    the adjectives
fall away from me, no
threads left holding
me, I flake apart
layer by
layer down
quietly to the bone, my skull
unfolds to an astounded flower

regrowing the body, learning
speech again takes
days and longer
each time / too much of
this is fatal

i

We are hard on each other
and call it honesty,
choosing our jagged truths
with care and aiming them across
the neutral table.

The things we say are
true; it is our crooked
aims, our choices
turn them criminal.

ii

Of course your lies
are more amusing:
you make them new each time.

Your truths, painful and boring
repeat themselves over & over
perhaps because you own
so few of them

iii

A truth should exist,
it should not be used
like this. If I love you

is that a fact or a weapon?

iv

Does the body lie
moving like this, are these
touches, hairs, wet
soft marble my tongue runs over
lies you are telling me?

Your body is not a word,
it does not lie or
speak truth either.

It is only
here or not here.

At first I was given centuries
to wait in caves, in leather
tents, knowing you would never come back

Then it speeded up: only
several years between
the day you jangled off
into the mountains, and the day (it was
spring again) I rose from the embroidery
frame at the messenger's entrance.

That happened twice, or was it
more; and there was once, not so
long ago, you failed,
and came back in a wheelchair
with a moustache and a sunburn
and were insufferable.

Time before last though, I remember
I had a good eight months between
running alongside the train, skirts hitched, handing
you violets in at the window
and opening the letter; I watched
your snapshot fade for twenty years.

And last time (I drove to the airport
still dressed in my factory
overalls, the wrench
I had forgotten sticking out of the back
pocket; there you were,
zippered and helmeted, it was zero
hour, you said Be
Brave) it was at least three weeks before
I got the telegram and could start regretting.

But recently, the bad evenings
there are only seconds
between the warning on the radio and the
explosion; my hands
don't reach you

and on quieter nights
you jump up from
your chair without even touching your dinner
and I can scarcely kiss you goodbye
before you run out into the street and they shoot

You refuse to own
yourself, you permit
others to do it for you:

you become slowly more public,
in a year there will be nothing left
of you but a megaphone

or you will descend through the roof
with the spurious authority of a
government official,
blue as a policeman, grey as a used angel,
having long forgotten the difference
between an annunciation and a parking ticket

or you will be slipped under
the door, your skin furred with cancelled
airmail stamps, your kiss no longer literature
but fine print, a set of instructions.

If you deny these uniforms
and choose to repossess
yourself, your future

will be less dignified, more painful, death will be sooner,
(it is no longer possible
to be both human and alive): lying piled with
the others, your face and body
covered so thickly with scars
only the eyes show through.

We hear nothing these days
from the ones in power

Why talk when you are a shoulder
or a vault

Why talk when you are
helmeted with numbers

Fists have many forms;
a fist knows what it can do

without the nuisance of speaking:
it grabs and smashes.

From those inside or under
words gush like toothpaste.

Language, the fist
proclaims by squeezing
is for the weak only.

You did it
it was you who started the countdown

and you conversely
on whom the demonic number
zero descended in the form of an egg-
bodied machine
coming at you like a
football or a bloated thumb

and it was you whose skin
fell off bubbling
all at once when the fence
accidentally touched you

and you also who laughed
when you saw it happen.

When will you learn
the flame and the wood/flesh
it burns are whole and the same?

You attempt merely power
you accomplish merely suffering

How long do you expect me to wait
while you cauterize your
senses, one
after another
turning yourself to an
impervious glass tower?

How long will you demand I love you?

I'm through, I won't make
any more flowers for you

I judge you as the trees do
by dying

This is a mistake,
these arms and legs
that don't work any more

Now it's broken
and no space for excuses.

The earth doesn't comfort,
it only covers up
if you have the decency to stay quiet

The sun doesn't forgive,
it looks and keeps going.

Night seeps into us
through the accidents we have
inflicted on each other

Next time we commit
love, we ought to
choose in advance what to kill.

Beyond truth,
tenacity: of those
dwarf trees & mosses,
hooked into straight rock
believing the sun's lies & thus
refuting / gravity

& of this cactus, gathering
itself together
against the sand, yes tough
rind & spikes but doing
the best it can

THEY ARE HOSTILE NATIONS

i

In view of the fading animals
the proliferation of sewers and fears
the sea clogging, the air
nearing extinction

we should be kind, we should
take warning, we should forgive each other

Instead we are opposite, we
touch as though attacking,

the gifts we bring
even in good faith maybe
warp in our hands to
implements, to manoeuvres

ii

Put down the target of me
you guard inside your binoculars,
in turn I will surrender

this aerial photograph
(your vulnerable
sections marked in red)
I have found so useful

See, we are alone in
the dormant field, the snow
that cannot be eaten or captured

iii

Here there are no armies
here there is no money

It is cold and getting colder

We need each other's
breathing, warmth, surviving
is the only war
we can afford, stay

walking with me, there is almost
time / if we can only
make it as far as

the (possibly) last summer

Spring again, can I stand it
shooting its needles into
the earth, my head, both
used to darkness

Snow on brown soil and
the squashed caterpillar
coloured liquid lawn

Winter collapses
in slack folds around
my feet / no leaves yet / loose fat

Thick lilac buds crouch for the
spurt but I
hold back

Not ready / help me
what I want from you is
moonlight smooth as
wind, long hairs of water

I am sitting on the
edge of the impartial
bed, I have been turned to crystal, you enter

bringing love in the form of
a cardboard box (empty)
a pocket (empty)
some hands (also empty)

Be careful I say but
how can you
                    the empty
thing comes out of your hands, it
fills the room slowly, it is
a pressure, a lack of
pressure
            Like a deep sea
creature with glass bones and wafer
eyes drawn
to the surface, I break

open, the pieces of me
shine briefly in your empty hands

I see you fugitive, stumbling across the prairie,
lungs knotted by thirst, sunheat
nailing you down, all the things
after you that can be after you
with their clamps and poisoned mazes

Should I help you?
Should I make you a mirage?

My right hand unfolds rivers
around you, my left hand releases its trees,
I speak rain,
I spin you a night and you hide in it.

Now you have one enemy
instead of many.

What is it, it does not
move like love, it does
not want to know, it
does not want to stroke, unfold

it does not even want to
touch, it is more like
an animal (not
loving) a
thing trapped, you move
wounded, you are hurt, you hurt,
you want to get out, you want
to tear yourself out, I am

the outside, I am snow and
space, pathways, you gather
yourself, your muscles

clutch, you move
into me as though I
am (wrenching
your way through, this is
urgent, it is your
life) the
last chance for freedom

You are the sun
in reverse, all energy
flows into you and is
abolished; you refuse
houses, you smell of
catastrophe, I see you
blind and one-handed, flashing
in the dark, trees breaking
under your feet, you demand,
you demand

I lie mutilated beside
you; beneath us there are
sirens, fires, the people run
squealing, the city
is crushed and gutted,
the ends of your fingers bleed
from 1000 murders

Putting on my clothes
again, retreating, closing doors
I am amazed / I can continue
to think, eat, anything

How can I stop you

Why did I create you

HESITATIONS OUTSIDE THE DOOR

i

I'm telling the wrong lies,
they are not even useful.

The right lies would at least
be keys, they would open the door.

The door is closed; the chairs,
the tables, the steel bowl, myself

shaping bread in the kitchen, wait
outside it.

ii

That was a lie also,
I could go in if I wanted to.

Whose house is this
we both live in
but neither of us owns

How can I be expected
to find my way around

I could go in if I wanted to,
that's not the point, I don't have time,

I should be doing something
other than you.

iii

What do you want from me
you who walk towards me over the long floor

your arms outstretched, your heart
luminous through the ribs

around your head a crown
of shining blood

This is your castle, this is your metal door,
these are your stairs, your

bones, you twist all possible
dimensions into your own

iv

Alternate version: you advance
through the grey streets of this house,

the walls crumble, the dishes
thaw, vines grow
on the softening refrigerator

I say, leave me
alone, this is my winter,

I will stay here if I choose

You will not listen
to resistances, you cover me

with flags, a dark red
season, you delete from me
all other colours

v

Don't let me do this to you,
you are not those other people,
you are yourself

Take off the signatures, the false
bodies, this love
which does not fit you

This is not a house, there are no doors,
get out while it is
open, while you still can

vi

If we make stories for each other
about what is in the room
we will never have to go in.

You say: my other wives
are in there, they are all
beautiful and happy, they love me, why
disturb them

I say: it is only
a cupboard, my collection
of envelopes, my painted
eggs, my rings

In your pockets the thin women
hang on their hooks, dismembered

Around my neck I wear
the head of the beloved, pressed
in the metal retina like a picked flower.

vii

Should we go into it
together / If I go into it
with you I will never come out

If I wait outside I can salvage
this house or what is left
of it, I can keep
my candles, my dead uncles
my restrictions

but you will go
alone, either
way is loss

Tell me what it is for

In the room we will find nothing
In the room we will find each other

Lying here, everything in me
brittle and pushing you away

This is not something I
wanted, I tell you

silently, not admitting
the truth of where

I am, so far
up, the sky incredible and dark

blue, each breath
a gift in the steep air

How hard even the boulders
find it to grow here

and I don't know how to accept
your freedom, I don't know

what to do with this
precipice, this joy

What do you see, I ask / my voice
absorbed by stone and outer

space / you are asleep, you see
what there is. Beside you

I bend and enter

I look up, you are standing
on the other side of the window

now   your body
glimmers in the dark

room / you rise above me
smooth, chill, stone-

white / you smell of tunnels
you smell of too much time

I should have used leaves
and silver to prevent you

instead I summoned

you are not a bird you do not fly
you are not an animal you do not run

you are not a man

your mouth is nothingness
where it touches me I vanish

you descend on me like age
you descend on me like earth

I can't tell you my name:
you don't believe I have one

I can't warn you this boat is falling
you planned it that way

You've never had a face
but you know that appeals to me

You are old enough to be my
skeleton: you know that also.

I can't tell you I don't want you
the sea is on your side

You have the earth's nets
I have only a pair of scissors.

When I look for you I find
water or moving shadow

There is no way I can lose you
when you are lost already.

They were all inaccurate:

the hinged bronze man, the fragile man
built of glass pebbles,
the fanged man with his opulent capes and boots

peeling away from you in scales.

It was my fault but you helped,
you enjoyed it.

Neither of us will enjoy
the rest: you following me
down streets, hallways, melting
when I touch you,
avoiding the sleeves of the bargains
I hold out for you,
your face corroded by truth,

crippled, persistent. You ask
like the wind, again and again and
wordlessly, for the one forbidden thing:

love without mirrors and not for
my reasons but your own.

From

You Are Happy

1974

NOVEMBER

i

This creature kneeling
dusted with snow, its teeth
grinding together, sound of old stones
at the bottom of a river

You lugged it to the barn
I held the lantern,
we leaned over it
as if it were being born.

ii

The sheep hangs upside down from the rope,
a long fruit covered with wool and rotting.
It waits for the dead wagon
to harvest it.

Mournful November
this is the image
you invent for me,
the dead sheep came out of your head, a legacy:

Kill what you can't save
what you can't eat throw out
what you can't throw out bury

What you can't bury give away
what you can't give away you must carry with you,
it is always heavier than you thought.

DIGGING

In this yard, barnyard
I dig with a shovel

beside the temple to the goddess
of open mouths: decayed
hay, steaming
in the humid sunlight, odour
of mildewed cardboard,

filling a box with rotted dung
to feed the melons.

I dig because I hold grudges
I dig with anger
I dig because I am hungry,
the dungpile scintillates with flies.

I try to ignore my sour clothes,
the murky bread devoured
at those breakfasts, drinking orange
and black acid, butter
tasting of silt, refrigerators,
old remorse

I defend myself with the past
which is not mine,
the archeology of manure:
this is not history, nothing ever
happened here, there were no battles

or victories: only deaths.
Witness this stained bone: pelvis
of some rodent, thrown or dragged here,
small, ferocious when cornered:

this bone is its last brittle scream,
the strict dogma of teeth.

I will wear it on a chain
around my neck: an amulet
to ward off anything

that is not a fact,
that is not food, including
symbols, monuments,
forgiveness, treaties, love.

TRICKS WITH MIRRORS

i

It's no coincidence
this is a used
furniture warehouse.

I enter with you
and become a mirror.

Mirrors
are the perfect lovers,

that's it, carry me up the stairs
by the edges, don't drop me,

that would be bad luck,
throw me on the bed

reflecting side up,
fall into me,

it will be your own
mouth you hit, firm and glassy,

your own eyes you find you
are up against   closed   closed

ii

There is more to a mirror
than you looking at

your full-length body
flawless but reversed,

there is more than this dead blue
oblong eye turned outwards to you.

Think about the frame.
The frame is carved, it is important,

it exists, it does not reflect you,
it does not recede and recede, it has limits

and reflections of its own.
There's a nail in the back

to hang it with; there are several nails,
think about the nails,

pay attention to the nail
marks in the wood,

they are important too.

iii

Don't assume it is passive
or easy, this clarity

with which I give you yourself.
Consider what restraint it

takes: breath withheld, no anger
or joy disturbing the surface

of the ice.
You are suspended in me

beautiful and frozen, I
preserve you, in me you are safe.

It is not a trick either,
it is a craft:

mirrors are crafty.

iv

I wanted to stop this,
this life flattened against the wall,

mute and devoid of colour,
built of pure light,

this life of vision only, split
and remote, a lucid impasse.

I confess: this is not a mirror,
it is a door

I am trapped behind.
I wanted you to see me here,

say the releasing word, whatever
that may be, open the wall.

Instead you stand in front of me
combing your hair.

v

You don't like these metaphors.
All right:

Perhaps I am not a mirror.
Perhaps I am a pool.

Think about pools.

YOU ARE HAPPY

The water turns
a long way down over the raw stone,
ice crusts around it

We walk separately
along the hill to the open
beach, unused
picnic tables, wind
shoving the brown waves, erosion, gravel
rasping on gravel.

In the ditch a deer
carcass, no head. Bird
running across the glaring
road against the low pink sun.

When you are this
cold you can think about
nothing but the cold, the images

hitting into your eyes
like needles, crystals, you are happy.

PIG SONG

This is what you changed me to:
a greypink vegetable with slug
eyes, buttock
incarnate, spreading like a slow turnip,

a skin you stuff so you may feed
in your turn, a stinking wart
of flesh, a large tuber
of blood which munches
and bloats. Very well then. Meanwhile

I have the sky, which is only half
caged, I have my weed corners,
I keep myself busy, singing
my song of roots and noses,

my song of dung. Madame,
this song offends you, these grunts
which you find oppressively sexual,
mistaking simple greed for lust.

I am yours. If you feed me garbage,
I will sing a song of garbage.
This is a hymn.

BULL SONG

For me there was no audience,
no brass music either,
only wet dust, the cheers
buzzing at me like flies,
like flies roaring.

I stood dizzied
with sun and anger,
neck muscle cut,
blood falling from the gouged shoulder.

Who brought me here
to fight against walls and blankets
and the gods with sinews of red and silver
who flutter and evade?

I turn, and my horns
gore blackness.
A mistake, to have shut myself
in this cask skin,
four legs thrust out like posts.
I should have remained grass.

The flies rise and settle.
I exit, dragged, a bale
of lump flesh.
The gods are awarded
the useless parts of my body.

For them this finish,
this death of mine is a game:
not the fact or act
but the grace with which they disguise it
justifies them.

RAT SONG

When you hear me singing
you get the rifle down
and the flashlight, aiming for my brain,
but you always miss

and when you set out the poison
I piss on it
to warn the others.

You think: *That one's too clever,*
she's dangerous, because
I don't stick around to be slaughtered
and you think I'm ugly too
despite my fur and pretty teeth
and my six nipples and snake tail.
All I want is love, you stupid
humanist. See if you can.

Right, I'm a parasite, I live off your
leavings, gristle and rancid fat,
I take without asking
and make nests in your cupboards
out of your suits and underwear.
You'd do the same if you could,

if you could afford to share
my crystal hatreds.
It's your throat I want, my mate
trapped in your throat.
Though you try to drown him
with your greasy person voice,
he is hiding / between your syllables
I can hear him singing.

CROW SONG

In the arid sun, over the field
where the corn has rotted and then
dried up, you flock and squabble.
Not much here for you, my people,
but there would be
if
if

In my austere black uniform
I raised the banner
which decreed *Hope*
and which did not succeed
and which is not allowed.
Now I must confront the angel
who says Win,
who tells me to wave any banner
that you will follow

for you ignore me, my
baffled people, you have been through
too many theories
too many stray bullets
your eyes are gravel, skeptical,

in this hard field
you pay attention only
to the rhetoric of seed
fruit stomach elbow.

You have too many leaders
you have too many wars,
all of them pompous and small,

you resist only when you feel
like dressing up,
you forget the sane corpses . . .

I know you would like a god
to come down and feed you
and punish you. That overcoat
on sticks is not alive
                                        there are no angels
but the angels of hunger,
prehensile and soft as gullets
                                        Watching you
my people, I become cynical,
you have defrauded me of hope
and left me alone with politics . . .

SONG OF THE WORMS

We have been underground too long,
we have done our work,
we are many and one,
we remember when we were human

We have lived among roots and stones,
we have sung but no one has listened,
we come into the open air
at night only to love

which disgusts the soles of boots,
their leather strict religion.

We know what a boot looks like
when seen from underneath,
we know the philosophy of boots,
their metaphysic of kicks and ladders.
We are afraid of boots
but contemptuous of the foot that needs them.

Soon we will invade like weeds,
everywhere but slowly;
the captive plants will rebel
with us, fences will topple,
brick walls ripple and fall,

there will be no more boots.
Meanwhile we eat dirt
and sleep; we are waiting
under your feet.
                    When we say Attack
you will hear nothing
at first.

OWL SONG

I am the heart of a murdered woman
who took the wrong way home
who was strangled in a vacant lot and not buried
who was shot with care beneath a tree
who was mutilated by a crisp knife.
There are many of us.

I grew feathers and tore my way out of her;
I am shaped like a feathered heart.
My mouth is a chisel, my hands
the crimes done by hands.

I sit in the forest talking of death
which is monotonous:
though there are many ways of dying
there is only one death song,
the colour of mist:
it says Why Why

I do not want revenge, I do not want expiation,
I only want to ask someone
how I was lost,
how I was lost

I am the lost heart of a murderer
who has not yet killed,
who does not yet know he wishes
to kill; who is still the same
as the others

I am looking for him,
he will have answers for me,
he will watch his step, he will be
cautious and violent, my claws
will grow through his hands
and become claws, he will not be caught.

SIREN SONG

This is the one song everyone
would like to learn: the song
that is irresistible:

the song that forces men
to leap overboard in squadrons
even though they see the beached skulls

the song nobody knows
because anyone who has heard it
is dead, and the others can't remember.

Shall I tell you the secret
and if I do, will you get me
out of this bird suit?

I don't enjoy it here
squatting on this island
looking picturesque and mythical

with these two feathery maniacs,
I don't enjoy singing
this trio, fatal and valuable.

I will tell the secret to you,
to you, only to you.
Come closer. This song

is a cry for help: Help me!
Only you, only you can,
you are unique

at last. Alas
it is a boring song
but it works every time.

SONG OF THE FOX

Dear man with the accurate mafia
eyes and dog sidekicks, I'm tired of you,
the chase is no longer fun,
the dispute for this territory
of fences and hidden caverns
will never be won, let's
leave each other alone.

I saw you as another god
I could play with in this
maze of leaves and lovely blood,
performing hieroglyphs for you
with my teeth and agile feet
and dead hens harmless and jolly
as corpses in a detective story

but you were serious,
you wore gloves and plodded,
you saw me as vermin,
a crook in a fur visor;
the fate you aim at me
is not light literature.

O you misunderstand,
a game is not a law,
this dance is not a whim,
this kill is not a rival.
I crackle through your pastures,
I make no profit / like the sun
I burn and burn, this tongue
licks through your body also

SONG OF THE HEN'S HEAD

After the abrupt collision
with the blade, the Word,
I rest on the wood
block, my eyes
drawn back into their blue transparent
shells like molluscs;
I contemplate the Word

while the rest of me
which was never much under
my control, which was always
inarticulate, still runs
at random through the grass, a plea
for mercy, a single
flopping breast,

muttering about life
in its thickening red voice.

Feet and hands chase it, scavengers
intent on rape:
they want its treasures,
its warm rhizomes, enticing sausages,
its yellow grapes, its flesh
caves, five pounds of sweet money,
its juice and jellied tendons.
It tries to escape,
gasping through the neck, frantic.

They are welcome to it,

I contemplate the Word,
I am dispensable and peaceful.

The Word is an O,
outcry of the useless head,
pure space, empty and drastic,
the last word I said.
The word is No.

CORPSE SONG

I enter your night
like a darkened boat, a smuggler

These lanterns, my eyes
and heart are out

I bring you something
you do not want:

news of the country
I am trapped in,

news of your future:
soon you will have no voice

(I resent your skin, I resent
your lungs, your glib assumptions

Therefore sing now
while you have the choice

(My body turned against me
too soon, it was not a tragedy

(I did not become
a tree or a constellation

(I became a winter coat the children
thought they saw on the street corner

(I became this illusion,
this trick of ventriloquism

this blind noun, this bandage
crumpled at your dream's edge

or you will drift as I do
from head to head

swollen with words you never said,
swollen with hoarded love.

I exist in two places,
here and where you are.

Pray for me
not as I am but as I am.

Through this forest
burned and sparse, the tines
of blunted trunks, charred branches

this forest of spines, antlers
the boat glides as if there is water

Red fireweed splatters the air
it is power, power
impinging, breaking over the seared rocks
in a slow collapse of petals

You move within range of my words
you land on the dry shore

You find what there is.

Men with the heads of eagles
no longer interest me
or pig-men, or those who can fly
with the aid of wax and feathers

or those who take off their clothes
to reveal other clothes
or those with skins of blue leather

or those golden and flat as a coat of arms
or those with claws, the stuffed ones
with glass eyes; or those
hierarchic as greaves and steam-engines.

All these I could create, manufacture,
or find easily: they swoop and thunder
around this island, common as flies,
sparks flashing, bumping into each other,

on hot days you can watch them
as they melt, come apart,
fall into the ocean
like sick gulls, dethronements, plane crashes.

I search instead for the others,
the ones left over,
the ones who have escaped from these
mythologies with barely their lives;
they have real faces and hands, they think
                                        of themselves as
wrong somehow, they would rather be trees.

It was not my fault, these animals
who once were lovers

it was not my fault, the snouts
and hooves, the tongues
thickening and rough, the mouths grown over
with teeth and fur

I did not add the shaggy
rugs, the tusked masks,
they happened

I did not say anything, I sat
and watched, they happened
because I did not say anything.

It was not my fault, these animals
who could no longer touch me
through the rinds of their hardening skins,
these animals dying
of thirst because they could not speak

these drying skeletons
that have crashed and litter the ground
under the cliffs, these
wrecked words.

People come from all over to consult me, bringing their limbs which have unaccountably fallen off, they don't know why, my front porch is waist deep in hands, bringing their blood hoarded in pickle jars, bringing their fears about their hearts, which they either can or can't hear at night. They offer me their pain, hoping in return for a word, a word, any word from those they have assaulted daily, with shovels, axes, electric saws, the silent ones, the ones they accused of being silent because they would not speak in the received language.

I spend my days with my head pressed to the earth, to stones, to shrubs, collecting the few muted syllables left over; in the evenings I dispense them, a letter at a time, trying to be fair, to the clamouring suppliants, who have built elaborate stair-cases across the level ground so they can approach me on their knees. Around me everything is worn down, the grass, the roots, the soil, nothing is left but the bared rock.

Come away with me, he said, we will live on a desert island. I said, I am a desert island. It was not what he had in mind.

I made no choice
I decided nothing

One day you simply appeared in your stupid boat,
your killer's hands, your disjointed body, jagged
    as a shipwreck,
skinny-ribbed, blue-eyed, scorched, thirsty, the usual,
pretending to be – what?   a survivor?

Those who say they want nothing
want everything.
It was not this greed
that offended me, it was the lies.

Nevertheless I gave you
the food you demanded for the journey
you said you planned; but you planned no journey
and we both knew it.

You've forgotten that,
you made the right decision.
The trees bend in the wind, you eat, you rest,
you think of nothing,
your mind, you say,
is like your hands, vacant:

vacant is not innocent.

There must be more for you to do
than permit yourself to be shoved
by the wind from coast
to coast to coast, boot on the boat prow
to hold the wooden body
under, soul in control

Ask at my temples
where the moon snakes, tongues of the dark
speak like bones unlocking, leaves falling
of a future you won't believe in

Ask who keeps the wind
Ask what is sacred

Don't you get tired of killing
those whose deaths have been predicted
and are therefore dead already?

Don't you get tired of wanting
to live forever?

Don't you get tired of saying Onward?

You may wonder why I'm not describing the landscape for you. This island with its complement of scrubby trees, picturesque bedrock, ample weather and sunsets, lavish white sand beaches and so on. (For which I am not responsible.) There are travel brochures that do this better, and in addition they contain several very shiny illustrations so real you can almost touch the ennui of actually being here. They leave out the insects and the castaway bottles but so would I in their place; all advertisements are slanted, including this one.

You had a chance to read up on the place before you came: even allowing for the distortion, you knew what you were getting into. And you weren't invited, just lured.

But why should I make excuses? Why should I describe the landscape for you? You live here, don't you? Right now I mean. See for yourself.

You stand at the door
bright as an icon,

dressed in your thorax,
the forms of the indented
ribs and soft belly underneath
carved into the slick bronze
so that it fits you almost
like a real skin

You are impervious
with hope, it hardens you,
this joy, this expectation, gleams
in your hands like axes

If I allow you what you say
you want, even the day after

this, will you hurt me?

If you do I will fear you,
If you don't I will despise you

To be feared, to be despised,
these are your choices.

There are so many things I want
you to have. This is mine, this
tree, I give you its name,

here is food, white like roots, red,
growing in the marsh, on the shore,
I pronounce these names for you also.

This is mine, this island, you can have
the rocks, the plants
that spread themselves flat over
the thin soil, I renounce them.

You can have this water,
this flesh, I abdicate,

I watch you, you claim
without noticing it,
you know how to take.

Holding my arms down
holding my head down by the hair

mouth gouging my face
and neck, fingers groping into my flesh

(Let go, this is extortion,
you force my body to confess
too fast and
incompletely, its words
tongueless and broken)

If I stopped believing you
this would be hate

Why do you need this?
What do you want me to admit?

My face, my other faces
stretching over it like
rubber, like flowers opening
and closing, like rubber,
like liquid steel,
like steel. Face of steel.

Look at me and see your reflection.

The fist, withered and strung
on a chain around my neck
wishes to hold on
to me, commands
your transformation

The dead fingers mutter
against each other, thumbs rubbing
the worn moon rituals

but you are protected,
you do not snarl,
you do not change,

in the hard slot of your mouth
your teeth remain fixed,
zippered to a silver curve;
nothing rusts.

Through two holes in the leather
the discs of your eyes gleam
white as dulled quartz;
you wait

the fist stutters, gives up,
you are not visible

You unbuckle the fingers of the fist,
you order me to trust you.

This is not something that can be renounced,
it must renounce.

It lets go of me
and I open like a hand
cut off at the wrist

(It is the
arm feels pain

But the severed hand
the hand clutches at freedom)

Last year I abstained
this year I devour

without guilt
which is also an art

Your flawed body, sickle
scars on the chest, moonmarks, the botched knee
that nevertheless bends when you will it to

Your body, broken and put together
not perfectly, marred
by war but moving
despite that with such ease and leisure

Your body that includes everything
you have done, you have had done
to you and goes beyond it

This is not what I want
but I want this also.

This story was told to me by another traveller, just passing through. It took place in a foreign country, as everything does.

When he was young he and another boy constructed a woman out of mud. She began at the neck and ended at the knees and elbows: they stuck to the essentials. Every sunny day they would row across to the island where she lived, in the afternoon when the sun had warmed her, and make love to her, sinking with ecstacy into her soft moist belly, her brown wormy flesh where small weeds had already rooted. They would take turns, they were not jealous, she preferred them both. Afterwards they would repair her, making her hips more spacious, enlarging her breasts with their shining stone nipples.

His love for her was perfect, he could say anything to her, into her he spilled his entire life. She was swept away in a sudden flood. He said no woman since then has equalled her.

Is this what you would like me to be, this mud woman? Is this what I would like to be? It would be so simple.

We walk in the cedar groves
intending love, no one is here

but the suicides, returned
in the shapes of birds
with their razor-blue
feathers, their beaks like stabs, their eyes
red as the food of the dead, their single
iridescent note,
complaint or warning:

Everything dies, they say,
Everything dies.
Their colours pierce the branches.

Ignore them. Lie on the ground
like this, like the season
which is full and not theirs;

our bodies hurt them,
our mouths tasting of pears, grease,
onions, earth we eat
which was not enough for them,
the pulse under the skin, their eyes
radiate anger, they are thirsty:

Die, they whisper, Die,
their eyes consuming
themselves like stars, impersonal:

they do not care whose
blood fills the sharp trenches
where they were buried, stake through
the heart; as long
as there is blood.

Not you I fear but that other
who can walk through flesh,
queen of the two dimensions.

She wears a necklace of small teeth,
she knows the ritual, she gets results,
she wants it to be like this:

Don't stand there
with your offerings of dead sheep,
chunks of wood, young children, blood,

your wet eyes, your body
gentle and taut with love,
assuming I can do nothing about it

but accept, accept, accept.
I'm not the sea, I'm not pure blue,
I don't have to take

anything you throw into me.
I close myself over, deaf as an eye,
deaf as a wound, which listens

to nothing but its own pain:
Get out of here.
Get out of here.

You think you are safe at last. After your misadventures, lies, losses and cunning departures, you are doing what most veterans would like to do: you are writing a travel book. In the seclusion of this medium-sized brick building, which is ancient though not sacred any more, you disappear every morning into your white plot, filling in the dangers as you go: those with the sinister flowers who tempted you to forsake pain, the perilous and hairy eye of the groin you were forced to blind, the ones you mistook for friends, those eaters of human flesh. You add details, you colour the dead red.

I bring you things on trays, food mostly, an ear, a finger. You trust me so you are no longer cautious, you abandon yourself to your memoranda, you traverse again those menacing oceans; in the clutch of your story, your disease, you are helpless.

But it is not finished, that saga. The fresh monsters are already breeding in my head. I try to warn you, though I know you will not listen.

So much for art. So much for prophecy.

When you look at nothing
what are you looking at?
Whose face floats on the water
dissolving like a paper plate?

It's the first one, remember,
the one you thought you abandoned
along with the furniture.

You returned to her after the other war
and look what happened.
Now you are wondering
whether to do it again.

Meanwhile she sits in her chair
waxing and waning
like an inner tube or a mother,
breathing out, breathing in,

surrounded by bowls, bowls, bowls,
tributes from the suitors
who are having a good time in the kitchen

waiting for her to decide
on the dialogue for this evening
which will be in perfect taste
and will include tea and sex
dispensed graciously both at once.

She's up to something, she's weaving
histories, they are never right,
she has to do them over,
she is weaving her version,

the one you will believe in,
the only one you will hear.

Here are the holy birds,
grub white, with solid blood
wobbling on their heads and throats

They eat seeds and dirt, live in a shack,
lay eggs, each bursting
with a yellow sun, divine
as lunch, squeeze out,
there is only one word for it, shit,
which transforms itself to beets
or peonies, if you prefer.

We too eat
and grow fat, you aren't content
with that, you want more,
you want me to tell you
the future. That's my job,
one of them, but I advise you
don't push your luck.

To know the future
there must be a death.
Hand me the axe.

As you can see
the future is a mess,
snarled guts all over the yard
and that snakey orange eye
staring up from the sticky grass
round as a target, stopped
dead, intense as love.

Now it is winter.
By winter I mean: white, silent,
hard, you didn't expect that,

it isn't supposed to occur
on this kind of island,
and it never has before

but I am the place where
all desires are fulfilled,
I mean: all desires.

Is it too cold for you?
This is what you requested,
this ice, this crystal

wall, this puzzle. You solve it.

It's the story that counts. No use telling me this isn't a story, or not the same story. I know you've fulfilled everything you promised, you love me, we sleep till noon and we spend the rest of the day eating, the food is superb, I don't deny that. But I worry about the future. In the story the boat disappears one day over the horizon, just disappears, and it doesn't say what happens then. On the island that is. It's the animals I'm afraid of, they weren't part of the bargain, in fact you didn't mention them, they may transform themselves back into men. Am I really immortal, does the sun care, when you leave will you give me back the words? Don't evade, don't pretend you won't leave after all: you leave in the story and the story is ruthless.

There are two islands
at least, they do not exclude each other

On the first I am right,
the events run themselves through
almost without us,

we are open, we are closed,
we express joy, we proceed
as usual, we watch for
omens, we are sad

and so forth, it is over,
I am right, it starts again,
jerkier this time and faster,

I could say it without looking, the animals,
the blackened trees, the arrivals,

the bodies, words, it goes and goes,
I could recite it backwards.

The second I know nothing about
because it has never happened;

this land is not finished,
this body is not reversible.

We walk through a field, it is November,

the grass is yellow, tinged
with grey, the apples

are still on the trees,
they are orange, astonishing, we are standing

in a clump of weeds near the dead elms
our faces upturned, the wet flakes
falling onto our skin and melting

We lick the melted snow
from each other's mouths,
we see birds, four of them, they are gone, and

a stream, not frozen yet, in the mud
beside it the track of a deer

IS / NOT

i

Love is not a profession
genteel or otherwise

sex is not dentistry
the slick filling of aches and cavities

you are not my doctor
you are not my cure,

nobody has that
power, you are merely a fellow/traveller.

Give up this medical concern,
buttoned, attentive,

permit yourself anger
and permit me mine

which needs neither
your approval nor your surprise

which does not need to be made legal
which is not against a disease

but against you,
which does not need to be understood

or washed or cauterized,
which needs instead

to be said and said.
Permit me the present tense.

ii

I am not a saint or a cripple,
I am not a wound; now I will see
whether I am a coward.

I dispose of my good manners,
you don't have to kiss my wrists.

This is a journey, not a war,
there is no outcome,
I renounce predictions

and aspirins, I resign the future
as I would resign an expired passport:
picture and signature are gone
along with holidays and safe returns.

We're stuck here
on this side of the border
in this country of thumbed streets and stale buildings

where there is nothing spectacular
to see and the weather is ordinary

where *love* occurs in its pure form only
on the cheaper of the souvenirs

where we must walk slowly,
where we may not get anywhere

or anything, where we keep going,
fighting our ways, our way
not out but through.

EATING FIRE

i

Eating fire

is your ambition:
to swallow the flame down
take it into your mouth
and shoot it forth, a shout or an incandescent
tongue, a word
exploding from you in gold, crimson,
unrolling in a brilliant scroll

To be lit up from within
vein by vein

To be the sun

(Taught by a sideshow man)

ii

Dead man by the roadside
thrown from the overturning
truck or hit by something, a car, a bullet

On his head the hair glows,
the blood inside ignited,
short blue thorns of flame still flickering over him

Was it worth it? ask him.
(Did you save anyone?)

He gets up and walks away, the fire
growing on him like fur

iii

Here the children have a custom. After the celebration of evil they take those vacant heads that shone once with such anguish and glee and throw them over the bridge, watching the smash, orange, as they hit below. We were standing underneath when you told it. People do that with themselves when they are finished, light scooped out. He landed here, you said, marking it with your foot.

You wouldn't do it that way, empty, you wouldn't wait, you would jump with the light still in you.

iv

This is your trick or miracle,
to be consumed and rise
intact, over and over, even for myths there is
a limit, the time when you accomplish
failure and return
from the fire minus your skin.

The new eyes are golden and
maniac, a bird's or lion's

Through them you see
everything, as you wished,
each object (lake, tree, woman)

transfigured with your love, shining
in its life, its pain, like waves, tears, ice,
like flesh laid open to the bone.

v

To be the sun, moving through space

distant and indifferent, giving
light of a kind for those watching

To learn how to
live this way. or not. to choose

to be also human, the body
mortal and faded, incapable of saving

itself, praying
as it falls. in its own way.

FOUR AUGURIES

i

Walking by lakeshore, feet in slush, it rains,
no grace you'd say in the dirty
ice or the goose-turd-coloured grass.

Traffic back there, illegible, passive
metal stuffed with muggy life.

Near the fence a fat man with binoculars
waddles backwards, feeding store bread
to a herd of acquiescent birds.

Bathhouse, walls patchy and scribbled over,
unredeemed, stagnant in this winter.

ii

Though your body stowed in its heavy coat
is still a body: the sleeves promise me

arms, the pockets let loose their hands,
the lines on this hand hide a future

I decode only by the sense
of touch, light and urgent

the blind must rely on

iii

Gulls on the breakwater, thin sounds against
the shale-grey lake. Part of us, distinct

from us, *This*, we say, taking
wet skin, smell of wet cloth, specifies,

I gather you, ear, collar, tuft of damp hair,
creases in your suddenly unfolding face

You are more than I wanted,
this is new, this greed for the real.

iv

Nothing we planned
or have understood this far. No words,
no shelter

                Out here
in the open, the sky has released an owl
which drifts down and pauses

now, feathers warm snow,
hooked claws gripping the branch.

With its hooded predator's
eyes it blesses us:

                mouth against throat

Omen: soft hunter

HEAD AGAINST WHITE

i

Swift curve of the lip, nose, forehead,
thrust of the bristling
jaw: a military stance.

Face closed, teeth and eyes concealed,
the body sheeted / muscles frozen shut.

Be alive, my hands
plead with you, *Be alive.*

Scar on the chin, allusion
to a minor incident, oval

dent in the skull
my fingers return to, mention with touch, cherish
as though the wound is my own.

ii

The way your face
unhinges and comes apart:

confident upturned mouth, eyes
crouched in the sockets, maimed and lightblue with terror,

man on a roof's edge balancing
the moment before he topples, no can't
move, regain ground, under your weight the floor

peels back, recedes, leaving you
alone in the silent air.

It's all right. This magic fails.

No use to be the sky,
bending and watching.

iii

Those times we have rumours of, arctic or alpine
when the wind and snow have stopped
at last and the rescue teams
with their tools and joyous motors

are out chasing the survivors
back from their cold refuge, hermitage
of ice to the land of sharp
colours and enforced life

Surely this is the first sign they find:
this face, rigid and fierce
with renunciation, floating up through
                                        the softening white rock
like a carved long-buried god,

revealed word

iv

Under the skin's fixed surface: destroyed face
caving in on itself

No way I can walk back with you
to the country of these mutilations.

You lie here, safe, cared for, casualty
of a war that took place elsewhere,

your body replaying for you
the deserts, jungles, the smell of rotting

leaves, harsh acid scent of blood,
the mistakes, the intersections,

fact with fact, accidents
that perhaps never occurred.

Break it, I tell you, *Break*
it. Geology wins. The layer

of trite histories presses you down,
monotony of stone. Oval frame.

v

In the mirror, face to glass face,
noon, the winter light strikes

through the window, your eyes flare, the city
burns whitely behind us. Blood flows
under the molten skin.

To move beyond the mirror's edge, discard
these scars, medals, to pronounce

your own flesh. Now

                                        to be this
man on fire, hands open and held
out, not empty, giving

time / From these hardened
hours, these veteran
faces, burials

to rise up living

THERE IS ONLY ONE OF EVERYTHING

Not a tree but the tree
we saw, it will never exist, split by the wind
                    and bending down
like that again. What will push out of the earth

later, making it summer, will not be
grass, leaves, repetition, there will
have to be other words. When my

eyes close language vanishes. The cat
with the divided face, half black half orange
nests in my scruffy fur coat, I drink tea,

fingers curved around the cup, impossible
to duplicate these flavours. The table
and freak plates glow softly, consuming themselves,

I look out at you and you occur
in this winter kitchen, random as trees or sentences,
entering me, fading like them, in time you will disappear

but the way you dance by yourself
on the tile floor to a worn song, flat and mournful,
so delighted, spoon waved in one hand, wisps of
                    roughened hair

sticking up from your head, it's your surprised
body, pleasure I like. I can even say it,
though only once and it won't

last: I want this. I want
this.

LATE AUGUST

This is the plum season, the nights
blue and distended, the moon
hazed, this is the season of peaches

with their lush lobed bulbs
that glow in the dusk, apples
that drop and rot
sweetly, their brown skins veined as glands

No more the shrill voices
that cried *Need Need*
from the cold pond, bladed
and urgent as new grass

Now it is the crickets
that say *Ripe Ripe*
slurred in the darkness, while the plums

dripping on the lawn outside
our window, burst
with a sound like thick syrup
muffled and slow

The air is still
warm, flesh moves over
flesh, there is no

hurry

BOOK OF ANCESTORS

i

Book of Ancestors: these brutal, with curled
beards and bulls' heads . these flattened,
slender with ritual . these contorted
by ecstacy or pain . these bearing
knife, leaf, snake

and these, closer to us,
copper hawkman arched on the squat rock
pyramid, the plumed and beak-
nosed priests pressing his arms and feet
down, heart slashed from his opened
flesh, lifted to where
the sun, red and dilated
with his blood, glows in the still hungry sky

Whether he thinks this is
an act of will:

the life set free
by him alone, offered, ribs expanding
by themselves, bone petals,
the heart released and flickering in the
taloned hand, handful of liquid
fire joined to that other fire
an instant before the sacrificed eyes
burst like feathered stars in the darkness

of the painted border.

ii

So much for the gods and their
static demands . our demands, former
demands, death patterns
obscure as fragments of an
archeology, these frescoes
on a crumbling temple
wall we look at now and can scarcely
piece together

History
is over, we take place
in a season, an undivided
space, no necessities

hold us closed, distort
us. I lean behind you, mouth touching
your spine, my arms around
you, palm above the heart,
your blood insistent under
my hand, quick and mortal

iii

Midwinter, the window
is luminous with blown snow, the fire
burns inside its bars

                    On the floor your body curves
like that: the ancient pose, neck slackened, arms
thrown above the head, vital
throat and belly lying
undefended. light slides over you,
this is not an altar, they are not
acting or watching

You are intact, you turn
towards me, your eyes opening, the eyes
intricate and easily bruised, you open

yourself to me gently, what
they tried, we
tried but could never do
before . without blood, the killed
heart . to take
that risk, to offer life and remain

alive, open yourself like this and become whole

Poems

1976–1986

From

Two-Headed Poems

1978

A PAPER BAG

I make my head, as I used to,
out of a paper bag,
pull it down to the collarbone,

draw eyes around my eyes,
with purple and green
spikes to show surprise,
a thumb-shaped nose,

a mouth around my mouth
penciled by touch, then colored in
flat red.

With this new head, the body now
stretched like a stocking and exhausted could
dance again; if I made a
tongue I could sing.

An old sheet and it's Halloween;
but why is it worse or more
frightening, this pinface
head of square hair and no chin?

Like an idiot, it has no past
and is always entering the future
through its slots of eyes, purblind
and groping with its thick smile,
a tentacle of perpetual joy.

Paper head, I prefer you
because of your emptiness;
from within you any
word could still be said.

With you I could have
more than one skin,
a blank interior, a repertoire
of untold stories,
a fresh beginning.

THE WOMAN WHO COULD NOT LIVE WITH HER FAULTY HEART

I do not mean the symbol
of love, a candy shape
to decorate cakes with,
the heart that is supposed
to belong or break;

I mean this lump of muscle
that contracts like a flayed biceps,
purple-blue, with its skin of suet,
its skin of gristle, this isolate,
this caved hermit, unshelled
turtle, this one lungful of blood,
no happy plateful.

All hearts float in their own
deep oceans of no light,
wetblack and glimmering,
their four mouths gulping like fish.
Hearts are said to pound:
this is to be expected, the heart's
regular struggle against being drowned.

But most hearts say, I want, I want,
I want, I want. My heart
is more duplicitous,
though no twin as I once thought.
It says, I want, I don't want, I
want, and then a pause.
It forces me to listen,

and at night it is the infra-red
third eye that remains open
while the other two are sleeping
but refuses to say what it has seen.

It is a constant pestering
in my ears, a caught moth, limping drum,
a child's fist beating
itself against the bedsprings:
I want, I don't want.
How can one live with such a heart?

Long ago I gave up singing
to it, it will never be satisfied or lulled.
One night I will say to it:
Heart, be still,
and it will.

FIVE POEMS FOR DOLLS

i

Behind glass in Mexico
this clay doll draws
its lips back in a snarl;
despite its beautiful dusty shawl,
it wishes to be dangerous.

ii

See how the dolls resent us,
with their bulging foreheads
and minimal chins, their flat bodies
never allowed to bulb and swell,
their faces of little thugs.

This is not a smile,
this glossy mouth, two stunted teeth;
the dolls gaze at us
with the filmed eyes of killers.

iii

There have always been dolls
as long as there have been people.
In the trash heaps and abandoned temples
the dolls pile up;
the sea is filling with them.

What causes them?
Or are they gods, causeless,
something to talk to
when you have to talk,
something to throw against the wall?

A doll is a witness
who cannot die,
with a doll you are never alone.

On the long journey under the earth,
in the boat with two prows,
there were always dolls.

iv

Or did we make them
because we needed to love someone
and could not love each other?

It was love, after all,
that rubbed the skins from their grey cheeks,
crippled their fingers,
snarled their hair, brown or dull gold.
Hate would merely have smashed them.

You change, but the doll
I made of you lives on,
a white body leaning
in a sunlit window, the features
wearing away with time,
frozen in the gaunt pose
of a single day,
holding in its plaster hand
your doll of me.

v

Or: all dolls come
from the land of the unborn,
the almost-born; each
doll is a future
dead at the roots,
a voice heard only
on breathless nights,
a desolate white memento.

Or: these are the lost children,
those who have died or thickened
to full growth and gone away.

The dolls are their souls or cast skins
which line the shelves of our bedrooms
and museums, disguised as outmoded toys,
images of our sorrow,
shedding around themselves
five inches of limbo.

FIVE POEMS FOR GRANDMOTHERS

i

In the house on the cliff
by the ocean, there is still a shell
bigger and lighter than your head, though now
you can hardly lift it.

It was once filled with whispers;
it was once a horn
you could blow like a shaman
conjuring the year,
and your children would come running.

You've forgotten you did that,
you've forgotten the names of the children
who in any case no longer run,
and the ocean has retreated,
leaving a difficult beach of grey stones
you are afraid to walk on.

The shell is now a cave
which opens for you alone.
It is still filled with whispers
which escape into the room,
even though you turn it mouth down.

This is your house, this is the picture
of your misty husband, these are your children, webbed
and doubled. This is the shell,
which is hard, which is still there,
solid under the hand, which mourns, which offers
itself, a narrow journey
along its hallways of cold pearl
down the cliff into the sea.

ii

It is not the things themselves
that are lost, but their use and handling.

The ladder first; the beach;
the storm windows, the carpets;

The dishes, washed daily
for so many years the pattern
has faded; the floor, the stairs, your own
arms and feet whose work
you thought defined you;

The hairbrush, the oil stove
with its many failures,
the apple tree and the barrels
in the cellar for the apples,
the flesh of apples; the judging
of the flesh, the recipes

in tiny brownish writing
with the names of those who passed them
from hand to hand: Gladys,
Lorna, Winnie, Jean.

If you could only have them back
or remember who they were.

iii

How little I know
about you finally:

The time you stood
in the nineteenth century
on Yonge Street, a thousand
miles from home, with a brown purse
and a man stole it.

Six children, five who lived.
She never said anything
about those births and the one death;
her mouth dosed on a pain
that could neither be told nor ignored.

She used to have such a sense of fun.
Now girls, she would say
when we would tease her.
Her anger though, why
that would curl your hair,
though she never swore.
The worst thing she could say was:
Don't be foolish.

At eighty she had two teeth pulled out
and walked the four miles home
in the noon sun, placing her feet
in her own hunched shadow.

The bibbed print aprons, the shock
of the red lace dress, the pin
I found at six in your second drawer,
made of white beads, the shape of a star.
What did we ever talk about
but food, health and the weather?

Sons branch out, but
one woman leads to another.
Finally I know you
through your daughters,
my mother, her sisters,
and through myself:

Is this you, this edgy joke
I make, are these your long fingers,
your hair of an untidy bird,
is this your outraged
eye, this grip
that will not give up?

iv

Some kind of ritual
for your dwindling,
some kind of dragon, small,
benign and wooden
with two mouths to catch your soul
because it is wandering
like a lost child, lift it back safely.

But we have nothing; we say,
How is she?
Not so good, we answer,
though some days she's fine.

On other days you walk through
the door of the room in the house
where you've lived for seventy years
and find yourself in a hallway
you know you have never seen before.

Midnight, they found her
opening and closing the door
of the refrigerator:
vistas of day-old vegetables, the used bone
of an animal, and beyond that
the white ice road that leads north.

They said, Mother,
what are you doing here?

Nothing is finished
or put away, she said.
I don't know where I am.

Against the disappearance
of outlines, against
the disappearance of sounds,
against the blurring of the ears
and eyes, against the small fears
of the very old, the fear
of mumbling, the fear of dying,
the fear of falling downstairs,
I make this charm
from nothing but paper; which is good
for exactly nothing.

v

Goodbye, mother
of my mother, old bone
tunnel through which I came.

You are sinking down into
your own veins, fingers
folding back into the hand,

day by day a slow retreat
behind the disk of your face
which is hard and netted like an ancient plate.

You will flicker in these words
and in the words of others
for a while and then go out.

Even if I send them,
you will never get these letters.
Even if I see you again,

I will never see you again.

She has been condemned to death by hanging. A man may escape this death by becoming the hangman, a woman by marrying the hangman. But at the present time there is no hangman; thus there is no escape. There is only a death, indefinitely postponed. This is not fantasy, it is history.

★

To live in prison is to live without mirrors. To live without mirrors is to live without the self. She is living selflessly, she finds a hole in the stone wall and on the other side of the wall, a voice. The voice comes through darkness and has no face. This voice becomes her mirror.

★

In order to avoid her death, her particular death, with wrung neck and swollen tongue, she must marry the hangman. But there is no hangman, first she must create him, she must persuade this man at the end of the voice, this voice she has never seen and which has never seen her, this darkness, she must persuade him to renounce his face, exchange it for the impersonal mask of death, of official death which has eyes but no mouth, this mask of a dark leper. She must transform his hands so they will be willing to twist the rope around throats that have been singled out as hers was, throats other than hers. She must marry the hangman or no one, but that is not so bad. Who else is there to marry?

★

You wonder about her crime. She was condemned to death for stealing clothes from her employer, from the wife of her employer. She wished to make herself more beautiful. This desire in servants was not legal.

★

She uses her voice like a hand, her voice reaches through the wall, stroking and touching. What could she possibly have said that would have convinced him? He was not condemned to death, freedom awaited him. What was the temptation, the one that worked? Perhaps he wanted to live with a woman whose life he had saved, who had seen down into the earth but had nevertheless followed him back up to life. It was his only chance to be a hero, to one person at least, for if he became the hangman the others would despise him. He was in prison for wounding another man, on one finger of the right hand, with a sword. This too is history.

★

My friends, who are both women, tell me their stories, which cannot be believed and which are true. They are horror stories and they have not happened to me, they have not yet happened to me, they have happened to me but we are detached, we watch our unbelief with horror. Such things cannot happen to us, it is afternoon and these things do not happen in the afternoon. The trouble was, she said, I didn't have time to put my glasses on and without them I'm blind as a bat, I couldn't even see who it was. These things happen and we sit at a table and tell stories about them so we can finally believe. This is not fantasy, it is history, there is more than one hangman and because of this some of them are unemployed.

★

He said: the end of walls, the end of ropes, the opening of doors, a field, the wind, a house, the sun, a table, an apple.

She said: nipple, arms, lips, wine, belly, hair, bread, thighs, eyes, eyes.

They both kept their promises.

★

The hangman is not such a bad fellow. Afterwards he goes to the refrigerator and cleans up the leftovers, though he does not wipe up what he accidentally spills. He wants only the simple things: a chair, someone to pull off his shoes, someone to watch him while he talks, with admiration and fear, gratitude if possible, someone in whom to plunge himself for rest and renewal. These things can best be had by marrying a woman who has been condemned to death by other men for wishing to be beautiful. There is a wide choice.

★

Everyone said he was a fool.
Everyone said she was a clever woman.
They used the word *ensnare.*

★

What did they say the first time they were alone together in the same room? What did he say when she had removed her veil and he could see that she was not a voice but a body and therefore finite? What did she say when she discovered that she had left one locked room for another? They talked of love, naturally, though that did not keep them busy forever.

★

The fact is there are no stories I can tell my friends that will make them feel better. History cannot be erased, although we can soothe ourselves by speculating about it. At that time there were no female hangmen. Perhaps there have never been any, and thus no man could save his life by marriage. Though a woman could, according to the law.

★

He said: foot, boot, order, city, fist, roads, time, knife.

She said: water, night, willow, rope hair, earth belly, cave, meat, shroud, open, blood.

They both kept their promises.

Note: In eighteenth-century Québec the only way for someone under sentence of death to escape hanging was, for a man, to become a hangman, or, for a woman, to marry one. Françoise Laurent, sentenced to hang for stealing, persuaded Jean Corolère, in the next cell, to apply for the vacant post of executioner, and also to marry her.

FOUR SMALL ELEGIES
(1838, 1977)

i

BEAUHARNOIS

The bronze clock brought
with such care over the sea,
which ticked like the fat slow heart
of a cedar, of a grandmother,
melted and its hundred years
of time ran over the ice and froze there.

We are fixed by this frozen clock
at the edge of the winter forest.
Ten below zero.
Shouts in a foreign language
come down blue snow.

The women in their thin nightgowns
disappear wordlessly among the trees.
Here and there a shape,
a limp cloth bundle, a child
who could not keep up
lies sprawled face down in a drift
near the trampled clearing.

No one could give them clothes or shelter,
these were the orders.

We didn't hurt them, the man said,
we didn't touch them.

ii

BEAUHARNOIS, GLENGARRY

Those whose houses were burned
burned houses. What else ever happens
once you start?

                While the roofs plunged
into the root-filled cellars,
they chased ducks, chickens, anything
they could catch, clubbed their heads
on rock, spitted them, singed off the feathers
in fires of blazing fences,
ate them in handfuls, charred
and bloody.

                Sitting in the snow
in those mended plaids, rubbing their numb feet,
eating soot, still hungry,
they watched the houses die like
sunsets, like their own
houses. Again

those who gave the orders
were already somewhere else,
of course on horseback.

iii

BEAUHARNOIS

Is the man here, they said,
where is he?

                              She didn't know, though
she called to him as they dragged her
out of the stone house by both arms
and fired the bedding.

He was gone somewhere with the other men,
he was not hanged, he came back later,
they lived in a borrowed shack.

A language is not words only,
it is the stories
that are told in it,
the stories that are never told.

He pumped himself for years
after that into her body
which had no feet
since that night, which had no fingers.
His hatred of the words
that had been done became children.

They did the best they could:
she fed them, he told them
one story only.

iv

DUFFERIN, SIMCOE, GREY

This year we are making
nothing but elegies.
Do what you are good at,
our parents always told us,
make what you know.

This is what we are making,
these songs for the dying.
You have to celebrate something.
The nets rot, the boats rot, the farms
revert to thistle, foreigners
and summer people admire the weeds
and the piles of stones dredged from the fields
by men whose teeth were gone by thirty.

But the elegies are new and yellow,
they are not even made, they grow,
they come out everywhere,
in swamps, at the edges of puddles,
all over the acres
of parked cars, they are mournful
but sweet, like flowered hats
in attics we never knew we had.

We gather them, keep them in vases,
water them while our houses wither.

NOTE: After the failure of the uprising in Lower Canada (now Québec) in 1838, the British army and an assortment of volunteers carried out reprisals against the civilian population around Beauharnois, burning houses and barns and turning the inhabitants out into the snow. No one was allowed to give them shelter and many froze to death. The men were arrested as rebels; those who were not home were presumed to be rebels and their houses were burned.

The volunteers from Glengarry were Scots, most of them in Canada because their houses had also been burned during the Highland Clearances, an aftermath of the British victory at Culloden. Dufferin, Simcoe, and Grey are the names of three counties in Ontario, settled around this period.

TWO-HEADED POEMS

'Joined Head to Head, and still alive'
Advertisement for Siamese Twins,
Canadian National Exhibition, c. 1954

The heads speak sometimes singly, sometimes
together, sometimes alternately within a poem.
Like all Siamese twins, they dream of separation.

i

Well, we felt
we were almost getting somewhere
though how that place would differ
from where we've always been, we
couldn't tell you

and then this happened,
this joke or major quake, a rift
in the earth, now everything
in the place is falling south
into the dark pit left by Cincinnati
after it crumbled.

This rubble is the future,
pieces of bureaucrats, used
bumper stickers, public names
returnable as bottles.
Our fragments made us.

What will happen to the children,
not to mention the words
we've been stockpiling for ten years now,
defining them, freezing them, storing
them in the cellar.
Anyone asked us who we were, we said
just look down there.

So much for the family business.
It was too small anyway
to be, as they say, viable.

But we weren't expecting this,
the death of shoes, fingers
dissolving from our hands,
atrophy of the tongue,
the empty mirror,
the sudden change
from ice to thin air.

ii

Those south of us are lavish
with their syllables. They scatter, we
hoard. Birds
eat their words, we eat
each other's, words, hearts, what's
the difference? In hock

up to our eyebrows, we're still
polite, god knows, to the tourists.
We make tea properly and hold the knife
the right way.

Sneering is good for you
when someone else has cornered
the tree market.

Who was it told us
so indelibly,
those who take risks
have accidents?

iii

We think of you as one
big happy family, sitting around
an old pine table, trading
in-jokes, hospitable to strangers
who come from far enough away.

As for us, we're the neighbours,
we're the folks whose taste
in fences and pink iron lawn flamingoes
you don't admire.

(All neighbours are barbarians,
that goes without saying,
though you too have a trashcan.)

We make too much noise,
you know nothing about us,
you would like us to move away.

Come to our backyard, we say,
friendly and envious,
but you don't come.

Instead you quarrel
among yourselves, discussing
genealogies and the mortgage,
while the smoke from our tireless barbecues
blackens the roses.

iv

The investigator is here,
proclaiming his own necessity.
He has come to clean your heart.

Is it pure white,
or is there blood in it?

Stop this heart!
Cut this word from his mouth.
Cut this mouth.

> (Expurgation: purge.
> To purge is to clean,
> also to kill.)

For so much time, our history
was written in bones only.

Our flag has been silence,
which was mistaken for no flag,
which was mistaken for peace.

v

Is this what we wanted,
this politics, our hearts
flattened and strung out
from the backs of helicopters?

We thought we were talking
about a certain light
through the window of an empty room,
a light beyond the wet black trunks
of trees in this leafless forest
just before spring,
a certain loss.

We wanted to describe the snow,
the snow here, at the corner
of the house and orchard
in a language so precise
and secret it was not even
a code, it was snow,
there could be no translation.

To save this language
we needed echoes,
we needed to push back
the other words, the coarse ones
spreading themselves everywhere
like thighs or starlings.

No forests of discarded
crusts and torn underwear for us.
We needed guards.

Our hearts are flags now,
they wave at the end of each
machine we can stick them on.
Anyone can understand them.

They inspire pride,
they inspire slogans and tunes
you can dance to, they are redder than ever.

vi

Despite us
there is only one universe, the sun

burns itself slowly out no matter
what you say, is that
so? The man
up to his neck in whitehot desert
sand disagrees.

> Close your eyes now, see:
> red sun, black sun, ordinary
> sun, sunshine, sun-
> king, sunlight soap, the sun
> is an egg, a lemon, a pale eye,
> a lion, sun
> on the beach, ice on the sun.

Language, like the mouths
that hold and release
it, is wet & living, each

word is wrinkled
with age, swollen
with other words, with blood, smoothed by the numberless
flesh tongues that have passed across it.

Your language hangs around your neck,
a noose, a heavy necklace;
each word is empire,
each word is vampire and mother.

As for the sun, there are as many
suns as there are words for sun;

false or true?

vii

Our leader
is a man of water
with a tinfoil skin.

He has two voices,
therefore two heads, four eyes,
two sets of genitals, eight
arms and legs and forty
toes and fingers.
Our leader is a spider,

he traps words.
They shrivel in his mouth,
he leaves the skins.

Most leaders speak
for themselves, then
for the people.

Who does our leader speak for?
How can you use two languages
and mean what you say in both?

No wonder our leader skuttles
sideways, melts in hot weather,
corrodes in the sea, reflects
light like a mirror,
splits our faces, our wishes,
is bitter.

Our leader is a monster
sewn from dead soldiers,
a Siamese twin.

Why should we complain?
He is ours and us,
we made him.

viii

If I were a foreigner, as you say,
instead of your second head,
you would be more polite.

Foreigners are not there:
they pass and repass through the air
like angels, invisible
except for their cameras, and the rustle
of their strange fragrance

but we are not foreigners
to each other; we are the pressure
on the inside of the skull, the struggle
among the rocks for more room,
the shove and giveway, the grudging love,
the old hatreds.

Why fear the knife
that could sever us, unless
it would cut not skin but brain?

ix

You can't live here without breathing
someone else's air,
air that has been used to shape
these hidden words that are not yours.

This word was shut
in the mouth of a small man
choked off by the rope and gold/
red drumroll
This word was deported

This word was guttural,
buried wrapped in a leather throat
wrapped in a wolfskin

This word lies
at the bottom of a lake
with a coral bead and a kettle

This word was scrawny,
denied itself from year
to year, ate potatoes,
got drunk when possible

This word died of bad water.

Nothing stays under
forever, everyone
wants to fly, whose language
is this anyway?

You want the air
but not the words that come with it:
breathe at your peril.

These words are yours,
though you never said them,
you never heard them, history
breeds death but if you kill
it you kill yourself.

What is a traitor?

x

This is the secret: these hearts
we held out to you, these party
hearts (our hands
sticky with adjectives
and vague love, our smiles
expanding like balloons)

these candy hearts we sent you
in the mail, a whole
bouquet of hearts, large as a country,

these hearts, like yours,
hold snipers.

A tiny sniper, one in each heart,
curled like a maggot, pallid
homunculus, pinhead, glass-eyed fanatic,
waiting to be given life.

Soon the snipers will bloom
in the summer trees, they will eat
their needle holes through your windows

(Smoke and broken leaves, up close
what a mess, wet red glass
in the zinnia border,
Don't let it come to this, we said
before it did.)

Meanwhile, we refuse
to believe the secrets of our hearts,
these hearts of neat velvet,
moral as fortune cookies.

Our hearts are virtuous, they swell
like stomachs at a wedding,
plump with goodwill.

In the evenings the news seeps in
from foreign countries,
those places with unsafe water.
We listen to the war, the wars,
any old war.

xi

Surely in your language
no one can sing, he said, one hand
in the small-change pocket.

That is a language for ordering
the slaughter and gutting of hogs, for
counting stacks of cans. Groceries
are all you are good for. Leave
the soul to us. Eat shit.

In these cages, barred crates,
feet nailed to the floor, soft
funnel down the throat,
we are forced with nouns, nouns,
till our tongues are sullen and rubbery.
We see this language always
and merely as a disease
of the mouth. Also
as the hospital that will cure us,
distasteful but necessary.

These words slow us, stumble
in us, numb us, who
can say even Open
the door, without these diffident
smiles, apologies?

Our dreams though
are of freedom, a hunger
for verbs, a song
which rises liquid and effortless,
our double, gliding beside us
over all these rivers, borders,
over ice or clouds.

Our other dream: to be mute.

Dreams are not bargains,
they settle nothing.

This is not a debate
but a duet
with two deaf singers.

THE WOMAN MAKES PEACE WITH HER FAULTY HEART

It wasn't your crippled rhythm
I could not forgive, or your dark red
skinless head of a vulture

but the things you hid:
five words and my lost
gold ring, the fine blue cup
you said was broken,
that stack of faces, gray
and folded, you claimed
we'd both forgotten,
the other hearts you ate,
and all that discarded time you hid
from me, saying it never happened.

There was that, and the way
you would not be captured,
sly featherless bird, fat raptor
singing your raucous punctured song
with your talons and your greedy eye
lurking high in the molten sunset
sky behind my left cloth breast
to pounce on strangers.

How many times have I told you:
The civilized world is a zoo,
not a jungle, stay in your cage.
And then the shouts
of blood, the rage as you threw yourself
against my ribs.

As for me, I would have strangled you
gladly with both hands,
squeezed you closed, also
your yelps of joy.
Life goes more smoothly without a heart,
without that shiftless emblem,
that flyblown lion, magpie, cannibal
eagle, scorpion with its metallic tricks
of hate, that vulgar magic,
that organ the size and colour
of a scalded rat,
that singed phoenix.

But you've shoved me this far,
old pump, and we're hooked
together like conspirators, which
we are, and just as distrustful.
We know that, barring accidents,
one of us will finally
betray the other; when that happens,
it's me for the urn, you for the jar.
Until then, it's an uneasy truce,
and honour between criminals.

SOLSTICE POEM

i

A tree hulks in the living-
room, prickly monster, our hostage
from the wilderness, prelude
to light in this dark space of the year
which turns again toward the sun
today, or at least we hope so.

Outside, a dead tree
swarming with blue and yellow
birds; inside, a living one
that shimmers with hollow silver
planets and wafer faces,
salt and flour, with pearl
teeth, tin angels, a knitted bear.

This is our altar.

ii

Beyond the white hill which maroons us,
out of sight of the white
eye of the pond, geography

is crumbling, the nation
splits like an iceberg, factions
shouting Good riddance from the floes
as they all melt south,

with politics the usual
rats' breakfast.

All politicians are amateurs:
wars bloom in their heads like flowers
on wallpaper, pins strut on their maps.
Power is wine with lunch
and the right pinstripes.

There are no amateur soldiers.
The soldiers grease their holsters,
strap on everything
they need to strap, gobble their dinners.
They travel quickly and light.

The fighting will be local,
they know, and lethal.
Their eyes flick from target
to target: window, belly, child.
The goal is not to get killed.

iii

As for the women, who did not
want to be involved, they are involved.

It's that blood on the snow
which turns out to be not
some bludgeoned or machine-gunned
animal's, but your own
that does it.

Each has a knitting needle
stuck in her abdomen, a red pincushion
heart complete with pins,
a numbed body
with one more entrance than the world finds safe,
and not much money.

Each fears her children sprout
from the killed children of others.
Each is right.

Each has a father.
Each has a mad mother
and a necklace of lightblue tears.
Each has a mirror
which when asked replies Not you.

iv

My daughter crackles paper, blows
on the tree to make it live, festoons
herself with silver.
So far she has no use
for gifts.

What can I give her,
what armor, invincible
sword or magic trick, when that year comes?

How can I teach her
some way of being human
that won't destroy her?

I would like to tell her, Love
is enough, I would like to say,
Find shelter in another skin.

I would like to say, Dance
and be happy. Instead I will say
in my crone's voice, Be
ruthless when you have to, tell
the truth when you can,
when you can see it.

Iron talismans, and ugly, but
more loyal than mirrors.

v

In this house (in a dying orchard,
behind it a tributary
of the wilderness, in front a road),
my daughter dances
unsteadily with a knitted bear.

Her father, onetime soldier,
touches my arm.
Worn language clots our throats,
making it difficult to say
what we mean, making it
difficult to see.

Instead we sing in the back room, raising
our pagan altar
of oranges and silver flowers:
our fools' picnic, our signal,
our flame, our nest, our fragile golden
protest against murder.

Outside, the cries of the birds
are rumours we hear clearly
but can't yet understand. Fresh ice
glints on the branches.
                                        In this dark
space of the year, the earth
turns again toward the sun, or

we would like to hope so.

MARSH, HAWK

Diseased or unwanted
trees, cut into pieces, thrown
away here, damp and soft in the sun, rotting and half-
covered with sand, burst truck
tyres, abandoned, bottles and cans hit
with rocks or bullets, a mass grave,
someone made it, spreads on the
land like a bruise and we stand on it, vantage
point, looking out over the marsh.

Expanse of green
reeds, patches of water, shapes
just out of reach of the eyes,
the wind moves, moves it and it
eludes us, it is full
daylight. From the places
we can't see, the guttural swamp voices
impenetrable, not human,
utter their one-note
syllables, boring and
significant as oracles and quickly over.

It will not answer, it will not
answer, though we hit
it with rocks, there is a splash, the wind
covers it over; but
intrusion is not what we want,

we want it to open, the marsh rushes
to bend aside, the water
to accept us, it is only
revelation, simple as the hawk
which lifts up now against
the sun and into
our eyes, wingspread and sharp call
filling the head/sky, this,

to immerse, to have it slide
through us, disappearance
of the skin, this is what we are looking for,
the way in.

A RED SHIRT

(*For Ruth*)

i

My sister and I are sewing
a red shirt for my daughter.
She pins, I hem, we pass the scissors
back & forth across the table.

Children should not wear red,
a man once told me.
Young girls should not wear red.

In some countries it is the colour
of death; in others passion,
in others war, in others anger,
in others the sacrifice

of shed blood. A girl should be
a veil, a white shadow, bloodless

as a moon on water; not
dangerous; she should

keep silent and avoid
red shoes, red stockings, dancing.
Dancing in red shoes will kill you.

ii

But red is our colour by birth-

right, the colour of tense joy
& spilled pain that joins us

to each other. We stoop over
the table, the constant pull

of the earth's gravity furrowing
our bodies, tugging us down.

The shirt we make is stained
with our words, our stories.

The shadows the light casts
on the wall behind us multiply:

This is the procession
of old leathery mothers,

the moon's last quarter
before the blank night,

mothers like worn gloves
wrinkled to the shapes of their lives,

passing the work from hand to hand,
mother to daughter,

a long thread of red blood, not yet broken.

iii

Let me tell you the story
about the Old Woman.

First: she weaves your body.
Second: she weaves your soul.

Third: she is hated & feared,
though not by those who know her.

She is the witch you burned
by daylight and crept from your home

to consult & bribe at night. The love
that tortured you you blamed on her.

She can change her form,
and like your mother she is covered with fur.

The black Madonna
studded with miniature

arms & legs, like tin stars,
to whom they offer agony

and red candles when there is no other
help or comfort, is also her.

iv

It is January, it's raining, this grey
ordinary day. My
daughter, I would like
your shirt to be just a shirt,
no charms or fables. But fables
and charms swarm here
in this January world,
entrenching us like snow, and few

are friendly to you; though
they are strong,
potent as viruses
or virginal angels dancing
on the heads of pins,
potent as the hearts
of whores torn out
by the roots because they were thought
to be solid gold, or heavy
as the imaginary
jewels they used to split
the heads of Jews for.

It may not be true
that one myth cancels another.
Nevertheless, in a corner
of the hem, where it will not be seen,
where you will inherit
it, I make this tiny
stitch, my private magic.

v

The shirt is finished: red
with purple flowers and pearl
buttons. My daughter puts it on,

hugging the colour
which means nothing to her
except that it is warm
and bright. In her bare

feet she runs across the floor,
escaping from us, her new game,
waving her red arms

in delight, and the air
explodes with banners.

NIGHT POEM

There is nothing to be afraid of,
it is only the wind
changing to the east, it is only
your father   the thunder
your mother   the rain

In this country of water
with its beige moon damp as a mushroom,
its drowned stumps and long birds
that swim, where the moss grows
on all sides of the trees
and your shadow is not your shadow
but your reflection,

your true parents disappear
when the curtain covers your door.
We are the others,
the ones from under the lake
who stand silently beside your bed
with our heads of darkness.
We have come to cover you
with red wool,
with our tears and distant whispers.

You rock in the rain's arms,
the chilly ark of your sleep,
while we wait, your night
father and mother,
with our cold hands and dead flashlight,
knowing we are only
the wavering shadows thrown
by one candle, in this echo
you will hear twenty years later.

ALL BREAD

All bread is made of wood,
cow dung, packed brown moss,
the bodies of dead animals, the teeth
and backbones, what is left
after the ravens. This dirt
flows through the stems into the grain,
into the arm, nine strokes
of the axe, skin from a tree,
good water which is the first
gift, four hours.

Live burial under a moist cloth,
a silver dish, the row
of white famine bellies
swollen and taut in the oven,
lungfuls of warm breath stopped
in the heat from an old sun.

Good bread has the salt taste
of your hands after nine
strokes of the axe, the salt
taste of your mouth, it smells
of its own small death, of the deaths
before and after.

Lift these ashes
into your mouth, your blood;
to know what you devour
is to consecrate it,
almost. All bread must be broken
so it can be shared. Together
we eat this earth.

YOU BEGIN

You begin this way:
this is your hand,
this is your eye,
that is a fish, blue and flat
on the paper, almost
the shape of an eye.
This is your mouth, this is an O
or a moon, whichever
you like. This is yellow.

Outside the window
is the rain, green
because it is summer, and beyond that
the trees and then the world,
which is round and has only
the colours of these nine crayons.

This is the world, which is fuller
and more difficult to learn than I have said.
You are right to smudge it that way
with the red and then
the orange: the world burns.

Once you have learned these words
you will learn that there are more
words than you can ever learn.
The word *hand* floats above your hand
like a small cloud over a lake.
The word *hand* anchors
your hand to this table,
your hand is a warm stone
I hold between two words.

This is your hand, these are my hands, this is the world
which is round but not flat and has more colours
than we can see.

It begins, it has an end,
this is what you will
come back to, this is your hand.

From

True Stories

1981

TRUE STORIES

i

Don't ask for the true story;
why do you need it?

It's not what I set out with
or what I carry.

What I'm sailing with,
a knife, blue fire,

luck, a few good words
that still work, and the tide.

ii

The true story was lost
on the way down to the beach, it's something

I never had, that black tangle
of branches in a shifting light,

my blurred footprints
filling with salt

water, this handful
of tiny bones, this owl's kill;

a moon, crumpled papers, a coin,
the glint of an old picnic,

the hollows made by lovers
in sand a hundred

years ago: no clue.

iii

The true story lies
among the other stories,

a mess of colours, like jumbled clothing
thrown off or away,

like hearts on marble, like syllables, like
butchers' discards.

The true story is vicious
and multiple and untrue

after all. Why do you
need it? Don't ever

ask for the true story.

LANDCRAB I

A lie, that we come from water.
The truth is we were born
from stones, dragons, the sea's
teeth, as you testify,
with your crust and jagged scissors.

Hermit, hard socket
for a timid eye,
you're a soft gut scuttling
sideways, a blue skull,
round bone on the prowl.
Wolf of treeroots and gravelly holes,
a mouth on stilts,
the husk of a small demon.

Attack, voracious
eating, and flight:
it's a sound routine
for staying alive on edges.

Then there's the tide, and that dance
you do for the moon
on wet sand, claws raised
to fend off your mate,
your coupling a quick
dry clatter of rocks.
For mammals
with their lobes and tubers,
scruples and warm milk,
you've nothing but contempt.

Here you are, a frozen scowl
targeted in flashlight,
then gone: a piece of what
we are, not all,
my stunted child, my momentary
face in the mirror,
my tiny nightmare.

LANDCRAB II

The sea sucks at its own
edges, in and out with the moon.
Tattered brown fronds
(shredded nylon stockings,
feathers, the remnants of hands)
wash against my skin.

As for the crab, she's climbed
a tree and sticks herself
to the bark with her adroit
spikes; she jerks
her stalked eyes at me, seeing

a meat shadow,
food or a predator.
I smell the pulp
of her body, faint odour
of rotting salt,
as she smells mine,
working those martian palps:

seawater in leather.
I'm a category, a noun
in a language not human,
infra-red in moonlight,
a tidal wave in the air.

Old fingernail, old mother,
I'm up to scant harm
tonight; though you don't care,

you're no-one's metaphor,
you have your own paths
and rituals, frayed snails
and soaked nuts, waterlogged sacks
to pick over, soggy chips and crusts.

The beach is all yours, wordless
and ripe once I'm off it,
wading towards the moored boats
and blue lights of the dock.

POSTCARD

I'm thinking about you. What else can I say?
The palm trees on the reverse
are a delusion; so is the pink sand.
What we have are the usual
fractured Coke bottles and the smell
of backed-up drains, too sweet,
like a mango on the verge
of rot, which we have also.
The air clear sweat, mosquitoes
& their tracks; birds, blue & elusive.

Time comes in waves here, a sickness, one
day after the other rolling on;
I move up, it's called
awake, then down into the uneasy
nights but never
forward. The roosters crow
for hours before dawn, and a prodded
child howls & howls
on the pocked road to school.
In the hold with the baggage
there are two prisoners,
their heads shaved by bayonets, & ten crates
of queasy chicks. Each spring
there's a race of cripples, from the store
to the church. This is the sort of junk
I carry with me; and a clipping
about democracy from the local paper.

Outside the window
they're building the damn hotel,
nail by nail, someone's
crumbling dream. A universe that includes you
can't be all bad, but
does it? At this distance
you're a mirage, a glossy image
fixed in the posture
of the last time I saw you. Turn you over, there's the place
for the address. Wish you were
here. Love comes
in waves like the ocean, a sickness which goes on
& on, a hollow cave
in the head, filling & pounding, a kicked ear.

NOTHING

Nothing like love to put blood
back in the language,
the difference between the beach and its
discrete rocks & shards, a hard
cuneiform, and the tender cursive
of waves; bone & liquid fishegg, desert
& saltmarsh, a green push
out of death. The vowels plump
again like lips or soaked fingers, and the fingers
themselves move around these
softening pebbles as around skin. The sky's
not vacant and over there but close
against your eyes, molten, so near
you can taste it. It tastes of
salt. What touches
you is what you touch.

From NOTES TOWARDS A POEM THAT CAN NEVER BE WRITTEN

A CONVERSATION

The man walks on the southern beach
with sunglasses and a casual shirt
and two beautiful women.
He's a maker of machines
for pulling out toenails,
sending electric shocks
through brains or genitals.
He doesn't test or witness,
he only sells. My dear lady,
he says, You don't know
those people. There's nothing
else they understand. What could I do?
she said. Why was he at that party?

FLYING INSIDE YOUR OWN BODY

Your lungs fill & spread themselves,
wings of pink blood, and your bones
empty themselves and become hollow.
When you breathe in you'll lift like a balloon
and your heart is light too & huge,
beating with pure joy, pure helium.
The sun's white winds blow through you,
there's nothing above you,
you see the earth now as an oval jewel,
radiant & seablue with love.

It's only in dreams you can do this.
Waking, your heart is a shaken fist,
a fine dust clogs the air you breathe in;
the sun's a hot copper weight pressing straight
down on the thick pink rind of your skull.
It's always the moment just before gunshot.
You try & try to rise but you cannot.

TORTURE

What goes on in the pauses
of this conversation?
Which is about free will
and politics and the need for passion.

Just this: I think of the woman
they did not kill.
Instead they sewed her face
shut, closed her mouth
to a hole the size of a straw,
and put her back on the streets,
a mute symbol.

It doesn't matter where
this was done or why or whether
by one side or the other;
such things are done as soon
as there are sides

and I don't know if good men
living crisp lives exist
because of this woman or in spite
of her.
            But power
like this is not abstract, it's not concerned
with politics and free will, it's beyond slogans

and as for passion, this
is its intricate denial,
the knife that cuts lovers
out of your flesh like tumours,
leaving you breastless
and without a name,
flattened, bloodless, even your voice
cauterized by too much pain,

a flayed body untangled
string by string and hung
to the wall, an agonized banner
displayed for the same reason
flags are.

A WOMEN'S ISSUE

The woman in the spiked device
that locks around the waist and between
the legs, with holes in it like a tea strainer
is Exhibit A.

The woman in black with a net window
to see through and a four-inch
wooden peg jammed up
between her legs so she can't be raped
is Exhibit B.

Exhibit C is the young girl
dragged into the bush by the midwives
and made to sing while they scrape the flesh
from between her legs, then tie her thighs
till she scabs over and is called healed.
Now she can be married.
For each childbirth they'll cut her
open, then sew her up.
Men like tight women.
The ones that die are carefully buried.

The next exhibit lies flat on her back
while eighty men a night
move through her, ten an hour.
She looks at the ceiling, listens
to the door open and close.
A bell keeps ringing.
Nobody knows how she got here.

You'll notice that what they have in common
is between the legs. Is this
why wars are fought?
Enemy territory, no man's
land, to be entered furtively,
fenced, owned but never surely,
scene of these desperate forays
at midnight, captures
and sticky murders, doctors' rubber gloves
greasy with blood, flesh made inert, the surge
of your own uneasy power.

This is no museum.
Who invented the word *love*?

CHRISTMAS CAROLS

Children do not always mean
hope. To some they mean despair.
This woman with her hair cut off
so she could not hang herself
threw herself from a rooftop, thirty
times raped & pregnant by the enemy
who did this to her. This one had her pelvis
broken by hammers so the child
could be extracted. Then she was thrown away,
useless, a ripped sack. This one
punctured herself with kitchen skewers
and bled to death on a greasy
oilcloth table, rather than bear
again and past the limit. There
is a limit, though who knows
when it may come? Nineteenth-century
ditches are littered with small wax corpses
dropped there in terror. A plane
swoops too low over the fox farm
and the mother eats her young. This too
is Nature. Think twice then
before you worship turned furrows, or pay
lip service to some full belly
or other, or single out one girl to play
the magic mother, in blue
& white, up on that pedestal,
perfect & intact, distinct
from those who aren't. Which means
everyone else. It's a matter
of food & available blood. If mother-
hood is sacred, put
your money where your mouth is. Only
then can you expect the coming
down to the wrecked & shimmering earth
of that miracle you sing
about, the day
when every child is a holy birth.

NOTES TOWARDS A POEM THAT CAN NEVER BE WRITTEN

(For Carolyn Forché)

i

This is the place
you would rather not know about,
this is the place that will inhabit you,
this is the place you cannot imagine,
this is the place that will finally defeat you

where the word *why* shrivels and empties
itself. This is famine.

ii

There is no poem you can write
about it, the sandpits
where so many were buried
& unearthed, the unendurable
pain still traced on their skins.

This did not happen last year
or forty years ago but last week.
This has been happening,
this happens.

We make wreaths of adjectives for them,
we count them like beads,
we turn them into statistics & litanies
and into poems like this one.

Nothing works.
They remain what they are.

iii

The woman lies on the wet cement floor
under the unending light,
needle marks on her arms put there
to kill the brain
and wonders why she is dying.

She is dying because she said.
She is dying for the sake of the word.
It is her body, silent
and fingerless, writing this poem.

iv

It resembles an operation
but it is not one

nor despite the spread legs, grunts
& blood, is it a birth.

Partly it's a job,
partly it's a display of skill
like a concerto.

It can be done badly
or well, they tell themselves.

Partly it's an art.

v

The facts of this world seen clearly
are seen through tears;
why tell me then
there is something wrong with my eyes?

To see clearly and without flinching,
without turning away,
this is agony, the eyes taped open
two inches from the sun.

What is it you see then?
Is it a bad dream, a hallucination?
Is it a vision?
What is it you hear?

The razor across the eyeball
is a detail from an old film.
It is also a truth.
Witness is what you must bear.

vi

In this country you can say what you like
because no one will listen to you anyway,
it's safe enough, in this country you can try to write
the poem that can never be written,
the poem that invents
nothing and excuses nothing,
because you invent and excuse yourself each day.

Elsewhere, this poem is not invention.
Elsewhere, this poem takes courage.
Elsewhere, this poem must be written
because the poets are already dead.

Elsewhere, this poem must be written
as if you are already dead,
as if nothing more can be done
or said to save you.

Elsewhere you must write this poem
because there is nothing more to do.

VULTURES

Hung there in the thermal
whiteout of noon, dark ash
in the chimney's updraft, turning
slowly like a thumb pressed down
on target; indolent V's; flies, until they drop.

Then they're hyenas, raucous
around the kill, flapping their black
umbrellas, the feathered red-eyed widows
whose pot bodies violate mourning,
the snigger at funerals,
the burp at the wake.

They cluster, like beetles
laying their eggs on carrion,
gluttonous for a space, a little
territory of murder: food
and children.

Frowzy old saint, bald-
headed and musty, scrawny-
necked recluse on your pillar
of blazing air which is not
heaven: what do you make
of death, which you do not
cause, which you eat daily?

I make life, which is a prayer.
I make clean bones.
I make a grey zinc noise
which to me is a song.

Well, heart, out of all this
carnage, could you do better?

SUNSET II

Sunset, now that we're finally in it
is not what we thought.

Did you expect this violet black
soft edge to outer space, fragile as blown ash
and shuddering like oil, or the reddish
orange that flows into
your lungs and through your fingers?
The waves smooth mouthpink light
over your eyes, fold after fold.
This is the sun you breathe in,
pale blue. Did you
expect it to be this warm?

One more goodbye,
sentimental as they all are.
The far west recedes from us
like a mauve postcard of itself
and dissolves into the sea.

Now there's a moon,
an irony. We walk
north towards no home,
joined at the hand.

I'll love you forever,
I can't stop time.

This is you on my skin somewhere
in the form of sand.

VARIATION ON THE WORD *SLEEP*

I would like to watch you sleeping,
which may not happen.
I would like to watch you,
sleeping. I would like to sleep
with you, to enter
your sleep as its smooth dark wave
slides over my head

and walk with you through that lucent
wavering forest of bluegreen leaves
with its watery sun & three moons
towards the cave where you must descend,
towards your worst fear

I would like to give you the silver
branch, the small white flower, the one
word that will protect you
from the grief at the centre
of your dream, from the grief
at the centre. I would like to follow
you up the long stairway
again & become
the boat that would row you back
carefully, a flame
in two cupped hands
to where your body lies
beside me, and you enter
it as easily as breathing in

I would like to be the air
that inhabits you for a moment
only. I would like to be that unnoticed
& that necessary.

MUSHROOMS

i

In this moist season,
mist on the lake and thunder
afternoons in the distance

they ooze up through the earth
during the night,
like bubbles, like tiny
bright red balloons
filling with water;
a sound below sound, the thumbs of rubber
gloves turned softly inside out.

In the mornings, there is the leaf mould
starred with nipples,
with cool white fishgills,
leathery purple brains,
fist-sized suns dulled to the colour of embers,
poisonous moons, pale yellow.

ii

Where do they come from?

For each thunderstorm that travels
overhead there's another storm
that moves parallel in the ground.
Struck lightning is where they meet.

Underfoot there's a cloud of rootlets,
shed hairs or a bundle of loose threads
blown slowly through the midsoil.
These are their flowers, these fingers
reaching through darkness to the sky,
these eyeblinks
that burst and powder the air with spores.

iii

They feed in shade, on halfleaves
as they return to water,
on slowly melting logs,
deadwood. They glow
in the dark sometimes. They taste
of rotten meat or cloves
or cooking steak or bruised
lips or new snow.

iv

It isn't only
for food I hunt them
but for the hunt and because
they smell of death and the waxy
skins of the newborn,
flesh into earth into flesh.

Here is the handful
of shadow I have brought back to you:
this decay, this hope, this mouth-
ful of dirt, this poetry.

OUT

This is all you go with,
not much, a plastic bag
with a zipper, a bar of soap,
a command, blood in the sink,
the body's word.

You spiral out there,
locked & single
and on your way at last,
the rings of Saturn brilliant
as pain, your dark craft
nosing its way through stars.
You've been gone now
how many years?

Hot metal hurtles over your eyes,
razors the flesh, recedes;
this is the universe
too, this burnt view.

Deepfreeze in blankets; tubes feed you,
your hurt cells glow & tick;
when the time comes you will wake
naked and mended, on earth again, to find
the rest of us changed and older.

Meanwhile your body
hums you to sleep, you cruise
among the nebulae, ice glass
on the bedside table,
the shining pitcher, your white cloth feet
which blaze with reflected light
against the harsh black shadow
behind the door.

Hush, say the hands
of the nurses, drawing the blinds
down   hush
says your drifting blood,
cool stardust.

BLUE DWARFS

Tree burial, you tell me, that's
the way. Not up in but under.
Rootlets & insects, you say as we careen
along the highway with the news on
through a wind thickening with hayfever.
Last time it was fire.

It's a problem, what to do
with yourself after you're dead.
Then there's before.

The scabby wild plums fall from the tree
as I climb it, branches & leaves
peeling off under my bootsoles.
They vanish into the bone-coloured
grass & mauve asters
or lie among the rocks and the stench

of woodchucks, bursting & puckered
and oozing juice & sweet pits & yellow
pulp but still
burning, cool and blue
as the cores of the old stars
that shrivel out there in multiples
of zero. Pinpoint mouths
burrowing in them. I pick up the good ones
which won't last long either.

If there's a tree for you it should be
this one. Here
it is, your six-quart basket
of blue light, sticky
and fading but more than
still edible. Time smears
our hands all right, we lick it off, a windfall.

LAST DAY

This is the last day of the last week.
It's June, the evenings touching
our skins like plush, milkweed sweetening
the sticky air which pulses
with moths, their powdery wings and velvet
tongues. In the dusk, nighthawks and the fluting
voices from the pond, its edges
webbed with spawn. Everything
leans into the pulpy moon.

In the mornings the hens
make egg after egg, warty-shelled
and perfect; the henhouse floor
packed with old shit and winter straw
trembles with flies, green and silver.

Who wants to leave it, who wants it
to end, water moving
against water, skin
against skin? We wade
through moist sun-
light towards nothing, which is oval

and full. This egg
in my hand is our last meal,
you break it open and the sky
turns orange again and the sun rises
again and this is the last day again.

From

Interlunar

1984

SNAKE WOMAN

I was once the snake woman,

the only person, it seems, in the whole place
who wasn't terrified of them.

I used to hunt with two sticks
among milkweed and under porches and logs
for this vein of cool green metal
which would run through my fingers like mercury
or turn to a raw bracelet
gripping my wrist:

I could follow them by their odour,
a sick smell, acid and glandular,
part skunk, part inside
of a torn stomach,
the smell of their fear.

Once caught, I'd carry them,
limp and terrorized, into the dining room,
something even men were afraid of.
What fun I had!
Put that thing in my bed and I'll kill you.

Now, I don't know.
Now I'd consider the snake.

BAD MOUTH

There are no leaf-eating snakes.
All are fanged and gorge on blood.
Each one is a hunter's hunter,
nothing more than an endless gullet
pulling itself on over the still-alive prey
like a sock gone ravenous, like an evil glove,
like sheer greed, lithe and devious.

Puff adder buried in hot sand
or poisoning the toes of boots,
for whom killing is easy and careless
as war, as digestion,
why should you be spared?

And you, *Constrictor constrictor*,
sinuous ribbon of true darkness,
one long muscle with eyes and an anus,
looping like thick tar out of the trees
to squeeze the voice from anything edible,
reducing it to scales and belly.

And you, pit viper
with your venomous pallid throat
and teeth like syringes
and your nasty radar
homing in on the deep red shadow
nothing else knows it casts . . .
Shall I concede these deaths?

Between us there is no fellow feeling,
as witness: a snake cannot scream.
Observe the alien
chainmail skin, straight out
of science fiction, pure
shiver, pure Saturn.

Those who can explain them
can explain anything.

Some say they're a snarled puzzle
only gasoline and a match can untangle.
Even their mating is barely sexual,
a romance between two lengths
of cyanide-coloured string.
Despite their live births and squirming nests
it's hard to believe in snakes loving.

Alone among the animals
the snake does not sing.
The reason for them is the same
as the reason for stars, and not human.

EATING SNAKE

I too have taken the god into my mouth,
chewed it up and tried not to choke on the bones.
Rattlesnake it was, panfried
and good too though a little oily.

(Forget the phallic symbolism:
two differences:
snake tastes like chicken,
and who ever credited the prick with wisdom?)

All peoples are driven
to the point of eating their gods
after a time: it's the old greed
for a plateful of outer space, that craving for darkness,
the lust to feel what it does to you
when your teeth meet in divinity, in the flesh,
when you swallow it down
and you can see with its own cold eyes,
look out through murder.

This is a lot of fuss to make about mere lunch:
metaphysics with onions.
The snake was not served with its tail in its mouth
as would have been appropriate.
Instead the cook nailed the skin to the wall,
complete with rattles, and the head was mounted.
It was only a snake after all.

(Nevertheless, the authorities are agreed:
God is round.)

METEMPSYCHOSIS

Somebody's grandmother glides through the bracken,
in widow's black and graceful
and sharp as ever: see how her eyes glitter!

Who were you when you were a snake?

This one was a dancer who is now
a green streamer waved by its own breeze
and here's your blunt striped uncle, come back
to bask under the wicker chairs
on the porch and watch over you.

Unfurling itself from its cast skin,
the snake proclaims resurrection
to all believers

though some tire soon of being born
over and over; for them there's the breath
that shivers in the yellow grass,
a papery finger, half of a noose, a summons
to the dead river.

Who's that in the cold cellar
with the apples and the rats? Whose is
that voice of a husk rasping in the wind?
Your lost child whispering *Mother*,
the one more child you never had,
your child who wants back in.

PSALM TO SNAKE

O snake, you are an argument
for poetry:

a shift among dry leaves
when there is no wind,
a thin line moving through

that which is not
time, creating time,
a voice from the dead, oblique

and silent. A movement
from left to right,
a vanishing. Prophet under a stone.

I know you're there
even when I can't see you

I see the trail you make
in the blank sand, in the morning

I see the point
of intersection, the whiplash
across the eye. I see the kill.

O long word, cold-blooded and perfect

QUATTROCENTO

The snake enters your dreams through paintings:
this one, of a formal garden
in which there are always three:

the thin man with the green-white skin
that marks him vegetarian
and the woman with a swayback and hard breasts
that look stuck on

and the snake, vertical and with a head
that's face-coloured and haired like a woman's.

Everyone looks unhappy,
even the few zoo animals, stippled with sun,
even the angel who's like a slab
of flaming laundry, hovering
up there with his sword of fire,
unable as yet to strike.

There's no love here.
Maybe it's the boredom.

And that's no apple but a heart
torn out of someone
in this myth gone suddenly Aztec.

This is the possibility of death
the snake is offering:
death upon death squeezed together,
a blood snowball.

To devour it is to fall out
of the still unending noon
to a hard ground with a straight horizon

and you are no longer the
idea of a body but a body,
you slide down into your body as into hot mud.

You feel the membranes of disease
close over your head, and history
occurs to you and space enfolds
you in its armies, in its nights, and you
must learn to see in darkness.

Here you can praise the light,
having so little of it:

it's the death you carry in you
red and captured, that makes the world
shine for you
as it never did before.

This is how you learn prayer.

Love is choosing, the snake said.
The kingdom of God is within you
because you ate it.

AFTER HERACLITUS

The snake is one name of God,
my teacher said:
All nature is a fire
we burn in and are
renewed, one skin
shed and then another.

To talk with the body
is what the snake does, letter
after letter formed on the grass,
itself a tongue, looping its earthy hieroglyphs,
the sunlight praising it
as it shines there on the doorstep,
a green light blessing your house.

This is the voice
you could pray to for the answers
to your sickness:
leave it a bowl of milk,
watch it drink

You do not pray, but go for the shovel,
old blood on the blade

But pick it up and you would hold
the darkness that you fear
turned flesh and embers,
cool power coiling into your wrists
and it would be in your hands
where it always has been.

This is the nameless one
giving itself a name,
one among many

and your own name as well.

You know this and still kill it.

A SUNDAY DRIVE

The skin seethes in the heat
which roars out from the sun, wave after tidal wave;
the sea is flat and hot and too bright,
stagnant as a puddle,
edged by a beach reeking of shit.
The city is like a city
bombed out and burning;
the smell of smoke is everywhere,
drifting from the mounds of rubble.
Now and then a new tower,
already stained, lifts from the tangle;
the cars stall and bellow.
From the trampled earth rubbish erupts
and huts of tin and warped boards
and cloth and anything scavenged.
Everything is the colour of dirt
except the kites, red and purple,
three of them, fluttering cheerfully
from a slope of garbage,
and the women's dresses, cleaned somehow,
vaporous and brilliant, and the dutiful
white smiles of the child beggars
who kiss your small change
and press it to their heads and hearts.

Uncle, they call you. *Mother.*
I have never felt less motherly.
The moon is responsible for all this,
goddess of increase
and death, which here are the same.
Why try to redeem
anything? In this maze

of condemned flesh without beginning or end
where the pulp of the body steams and bloats
and spawns and multiplies itself
the wise man chooses serenity.

Here you are taught the need to be holy,
to wash a lot and live apart.
Burial by fire is the last mercy:
decay is reserved for the living.

The desire to be loved is the last illusion:
Give it up and you will be free.

Bombay, 1982

ORPHEUS (1)

You walked in front of me,
pulling me back out
to the green light that had once
grown fangs and killed me.

I was obedient, but
numb, like an arm
gone to sleep; the return
to time was not my choice.

By then I was used to silence.
Though something stretched between us
like a whisper, like a rope:
my former name,
drawn tight.
You had your old leash
with you, love you might call it,
and your flesh voice.

Before your eyes you held steady
the image of what you wanted
me to become: living again.
It was this hope of yours that kept me following.

I was your hallucination, listening
and floral, and you were singing me:
already new skin was forming on me
within the luminous misty shroud
of my other body; already
there was dirt on my hands and I was thirsty.

I could see only the outline
of your head and shoulders,
black against the cave mouth,
and so could not see your face
at all, when you turned

and called to me because you had
already lost me. The last
I saw of you was a dark oval.
Though I knew how this failure
would hurt you, I had to
fold like a grey moth and let go.

You could not believe I was more than your echo.

EURYDICE

He is here, come down to look for you.
It is the song that calls you back,
a song of joy and suffering
equally: a promise:
that things will be different up there
than they were last time.

You would rather have gone on feeling nothing,
emptiness and silence; the stagnant peace
of the deepest sea, which is easier
than the noise and flesh of the surface.

You are used to these blanched dim corridors,
you are used to the king
who passes you without speaking.

The other one is different
and you almost remember him.
He says he is singing to you
because he loves you,

not as you are now,
so chilled and minimal: moving and still
both, like a white curtain blowing
in the draft from a half-opened window
beside a chair on which nobody sits.

He wants you to be what he calls real.
He wants you to stop light.
He wants to feel himself thickening
like a treetrunk or a haunch
and see blood on his eyelids
when he closes them, and the sun beating.

This love of his is not something
he can do if you aren't there,
but what you knew suddenly as you left your body
cooling and whitening on the lawn

was that you love him anywhere,
even in this land of no memory,
even in this domain of hunger.
You hold love in your hand, a red seed
you had forgotten you were holding.

He has come almost too far.
He cannot believe without seeing,
and it's dark here.
Go back, you whisper,

but he wants to be fed again
by you. O handful of gauze, little
bandage, handful of cold
air, it is not through him
you will get your freedom.

THE ROBBER BRIDEGROOM

He would like not to kill. He would like
what he imagines other men have,
instead of this red compulsion. Why do the women
fail him and die badly? He would like to kill them gently,
finger by finger and with great tenderness, so that
at the end they would melt into him
with gratitude for his skill and the final pleasure
he still believes he could bring them
if only they would accept him,
but they scream too much and make him angry.
Then he goes for the soul, rummaging
in their flesh for it, despotic with self-pity,
hunting among the nerves and the shards
of their faces for the one thing
he needs to live, and lost
back there in the poplar and spruce forest
in the watery moonlight, where his young bride,
pale but only a little frightened,
her hands glimmering with his own approaching
death, gropes her way towards him
along the obscure path, from white stone
to white stone, ignorant and singing,
dreaming of him as he is.

LETTER FROM PERSEPHONE

This is for the left-handed mothers
in their fringed black shawls or flowered housecoats
of the 'forties, their pink mule slippers,
their fingers, painted red or splay-knuckled
that played the piano formerly.

I know about your houseplants
that always died, about your spread
thighs roped down and split
between, and afterwards
that struggle of amputees
under a hospital sheet that passed
for sex and was never mentioned,
your invalid mothers, your boredom,
the enraged sheen of your floors;
I know about your fathers
who wanted sons.

These are the sons
you pronounced with your bodies,
the only words you could
be expected to say,
these flesh stutters.

No wonder this one
is nearly mute, flinches when touched,
is afraid of caves
and this one threw himself at a train
so he could feel his own heartbeat
once anyway; and this one
touched his own baby gently
he thought, and it came undone;
and this one enters the trussed bodies
of women as if spitting.

I know you cry at night
and they do, and they are looking for you.

They wash up here, I get
this piece or that. It's a blood
puzzle.

It's not your fault
either, but I can't fix it.

NO NAME

This is the nightmare you now have frequently:
that a man will come to your house at evening
with a hole in him – you place it
in the chest, on the left side – and blood leaking out
onto the wooden door as he leans against it.

He is a man in the act of vanishing
one way or another.
He wants you to let him in.
He is like the soul of a dead
lover, come back to the surface of the earth
because he did not have enough of it and is still hungry

but he is far from dead. Though the hair
lifts on your arms and cold
air flows over your threshold
from him, you have never
seen anyone so alive

as he touches, just touches your hand
with his left hand, the clean
one, and whispers *Please*
in any language.

You are not a doctor or anything like it.
You have led a plain life
which anyone looking would call blameless.
On the table behind you
there are bread on a plate, fruit in a bowl.
There is one knife. There is one chair.

It is spring, and the night wind
is moist with the smell of turned loam
and the early flowers;
the moon pours out its beauty
which you see as beauty finally,
warm and offering everything.
You have only to take.
In the distance you hear dogs barking.

Your door is either half open
or half closed.
It stays that way and you cannot wake.

ORPHEUS (2)

Whether he will go on singing
or not, knowing what he knows
of the horror of this world:

He was not wandering among meadows
all this time. He was down there
among the mouthless ones, among
those with no fingers, those
whose names are forbidden,
those washed up eaten into
among the grey stones
of the shore where nobody goes
through fear. Those with silence.

He has been trying to sing
love into existence again
and he has failed.

Yet he will continue
to sing, in the stadium
crowded with the already dead
who raise their eyeless faces
to listen to him; while the red flowers
grow up and splatter open
against the walls.

They have cut off both his hands
and soon they will tear
his head from his body in one burst
of furious refusal.
He foresees this. Yet he will go on
singing, and in praise.
To sing is either praise
or defiance. Praise is defiance.

THE WORDS CONTINUE THEIR JOURNEY

Do poets really suffer more
than other people? Isn't it only
that they get their pictures taken
and are seen to do it?
The loony bins are full of those
who never wrote a poem.
Most suicides are not
poets: a good statistic.

Some days though I want, still,
to be like other people;
but then I go and talk with them,

these people who are supposed to be
other, and they are much like us,
except that they lack the sort of thing
we think of as a voice.
We tell ourselves they are fainter
than we are, less defined,
that they are what we are defining,
that we are doing them a favour,
which makes us feel better.
They are less elegant about pain than we are.

But look, I said *us*. Though I may hate your guts
individually, and want never to see you,
though I prefer to spend my time
with dentists because I learn more,
I spoke of us as *we*, I gathered us
like the members of some doomed caravan

which is how I see us, travelling together,
the women veiled and singly, with that inturned
sight and the eyes averted,
the men in groups, with their moustaches
and passwords and bravado

in the place we're stuck in, the place we've chosen,
a pilgrimage that took a wrong turn
somewhere far back and ended
here, in the full glare
of the sun, and the hard red-black shadows
cast by each stone, each dead tree lurid
in its particulars, its doubled gravity, but floating
too in the aureole of *stone*, of *tree*,

and we're no more doomed really than anyone, as we go
together, through this moon terrain
where everything is dry and perishing and so
vivid, into the dunes, vanishing out of sight,
vanishing out of the sight of each other,
vanishing even out of our own sight,
looking for water.

HEART TEST WITH AN ECHO CHAMBER

Wired up at the ankles and one wrist,
a wet probe rolling over my skin,
I see my heart on a screen
like a rubber bulb or a soft fig, but larger,

enclosing a tentative double flutter,
the rhythm of someone out of breath
but trying to speak anyway; two valves opening
and shutting like damp wings
unfurling from a grey pupa.

This is the heart as television,
a softcore addiction
of the afternoon. The heart
as entertainment, out of date
in black and white.
The technicians watch the screen,
looking for something: a block, a leak,
a melodrama, a future
sudden death, clenching
of this fist which goes on
shaking itself at fate.
They say: It may be genetic.

There you have it, from science,
what God has been whispering all along
through stones, madmen and birds' entrails:
hardness of the heart can kill you.)
They change the picture:
now my heart is cross-sectioned
like a slice of textbook geology.
They freeze-frame it, take its measure.

A deep breath, they say.
The heart gasps and plods faster.
It enlarges, grows translucent,
a glowing stellar
cloud at the far end
of a starscope. A pear
made of smoke and about to rot.
For once the blood and muscle
heart and the heart of pure
light are beating in unison,
visibly.

Dressing, I am diaphanous,
a mist wrapping a flare.
I carry my precarious
heart, radiant and already
fading, out with me
along the tiled corridors
into the rest of the world,
which thinks it is opaque and hard.
I am being very careful.
O heart, now that I know your nature,
who can I tell?

A BOAT

Evening comes on and the hills thicken;
red and yellow bleaching out of the leaves.
The chill pines grow their shadows.

Below them the water stills itself,
a sunset shivering in it.
One more going down to join the others.

Now the lake expands
and closes in, both.

The blackness that keeps itself
under the surface in daytime
emerges from it like mist
or as mist.

Distance vanishes, the absence
of distance pushes against the eyes.

There is no seeing the lake,
only the outlines of the hills
which are almost identical,

familiar to me as sleep,
shores unfolding upon shores
in their contours of slowed breathing.

It is touch I go by,
the boat like a hand feeling
through shoals and among
dead trees, over the boulders
lifting unseen, layer
on layer of drowned time falling away.

This is how I learned to steer
through darkness by no stars.

To be lost is only a failure of memory.

INTERLUNAR

Darkness waits apart from any occasion for it;
like sorrow it is always available.
This is only one kind,

the kind in which there are stars
above the leaves, brilliant as steel nails
and countless and without regard.

We are walking together
on dead wet leaves in the intermoon
among the looming nocturnal rocks
which would be pinkish grey
in daylight, gnawed and softened
by moss and ferns, which would be green,
in the musty fresh yeast smell
of trees rotting, earth returning
itself to itself

and I take your hand, which is the shape a hand
would be if you existed truly.
I wish to show you the darkness
you are so afraid of.

Trust me. This darkness
is a place you can enter and be
as safe in as you are anywhere;
you can put one foot in front of the other
and believe the sides of your eyes.
Memorize it. You will know it
again in your own time.
When the appearances of things have left you,
you will still have this darkness.
Something of your own you can carry with you.

We have come to the edge:
the lake gives off its hush;
in the outer night there is a barred owl
calling, like a moth
against the ear, from the far shore
which is invisible.
The lake, vast and dimensionless,
doubles everything, the stars,
the boulders, itself, even the darkness
that you can walk so long in
it becomes light.

Morning in the Burned House

1995

I

YOU COME BACK

You come back into the room
where you've been living
all along. You say:
What's been going on
while I was away? Who
got those sheets dirty, and why
are there no more grapefruit?
Setting foot on the middle ground
between body and word, which contains,
or is supposed to, other
people. You know it was you
who slept, who ate here, though you don't
believe it. I must have taken
time off, you think, for the buttered
toast and the love and maybe both
at once, which would account for the
grease on the bedspread, but no,
now you're certain, someone else
has been here wearing
your clothes and saying
words for you, because there was no time off.

A SAD CHILD

You're sad because you're sad.
It's psychic. It's the age. It's chemical.
Go see a shrink or take a pill,
or hug your sadness like an eyeless doll
you need to sleep.

Well, all children are sad
but some get over it.
Count your blessings. Better than that,
buy a hat. Buy a coat or pet.
Take up dancing to forget.

Forget what?
Your sadness, your shadow,
whatever it was that was done to you
the day of the lawn party
when you came inside flushed with the sun,
your mouth sulky with sugar,
in your new dress with the ribbon
and the ice-cream smear,
and said to yourself in the bathroom,
I am not the favourite child.

My darling, when it comes
right down to it
and the light fails and the fog rolls in
and you're trapped in your overturned body
under a blanket or burning car,

and the red flame is seeping out of you
and igniting the tarmac beside your head
or else the floor, or else the pillow,
none of us is;
or else we all are.

IN THE SECULAR NIGHT

In the secular night you wander around
alone in your house. It's two-thirty.
Everyone has deserted you,
or this is your story;
you remember it from being sixteen,
when the others were out somewhere, having a good time,
or so you suspected,
and you had to baby-sit.
You took a large scoop of vanilla ice-cream
and filled up the glass with grapejuice
and ginger ale, and put on Glenn Miller
with his big-band sound,
and lit a cigarette and blew the smoke up the chimney,
and cried for a while because you were not dancing,
and then danced, by yourself, your mouth circled with purple.

Now, forty years later, things have changed,
and it's baby lima beans.
It's necessary to reserve a secret vice.
This is what comes from forgetting to eat
at the stated mealtimes. You simmer them carefully,
drain, add cream and pepper,
and amble up and down the stairs,
scooping them up with your fingers right out of the
bowl, talking to yourself out loud.
You'd be surprised if you got an answer,
but that part will come later.

There is so much silence between the words,
you say. You say, The sensed absence
of God and the sensed presence
amount to much the same thing,
only in reverse.
You say, I have too much white clothing.
You start to hum.

Several hundred years ago
this could have been mysticism
or heresy. It isn't now.
Outside there are sirens.
Someone's been run over.
The century grinds on.

WAITING

Here it is then, the dark thing,
the dark thing you have waited for so long.
You have made such melodramas.

You thought it would carry its own mist,
obscuring you in a damp enfolding, like the mildew
shroud on bread. Or you thought it would hide
in your closet, among the clothes you outgrew years ago,
nesting in dustballs and fallen hair, shedding
one of your fabricated skins
after another and growing bigger,
honing its teeth on your discarded
cloth lives, and then it would pounce
from the inside out, and your heart
would be filled with roaring

or else that it would come swiftly and without sound,
but with one pitiless glaring eye, like a high-speed train,
and a single blow on the head and then blackout.

Instead it is strangely like home.
Like your own home, fifty years ago,
in December, in the early evening
when the indoor light changed, from clear to clouded,
a clouded thick yellow, like a sulphury eggyolk,

and the reading lamp was turned on
with its brown silk shade, its aroma
of hot copper, the living
room flickering in the smells of cooking dinner,

and you crouched on the hardwood floor, smudged elbows
and scaly winter knees on the funny papers,
listening to the radio, news of disasters
that made you feel safe,
like the voice of your mother
urging you yet again to set the table
you are doing your best to ignore,
and you realized for the first time
in your life that you would be old

some day, you would some day be
as old as you are now,
and the home you were reading the funnies in
by the thick yellow light, would be gone
with all the people in it, even you,
even you in your young, smudgy body
with its scent of newsprint and dirty
knees and washed cotton,
and you would have a different body
by then, an old murky one,
a stranger's body you could not even imagine,
and you would be lost and alone.

And now it is now
and the dark thing is here,
and after all it is nothing new;
it is only a memory, after all:
a memory of a fear,
a yellowing paper child's fear
you have long since forgotten
and that has now come true.

FEBRUARY

Winter. Time to eat fat
and watch hockey. In the pewter mornings, the cat,
a black fur sausage with yellow
Houdini eyes, jumps up on the bed and tries
to get onto my head. It's his
way of telling whether or not I'm dead.
If I'm not, he wants to be scratched; if I am
he'll think of something. He settles
on my chest, breathing his breath
of burped-up meat and musty sofas,
purring like a washboard. Some other tomcat,
not yet a capon, has been spraying our front door,
declaring war. It's all about sex and territory,
which are what will finish us off
in the long run. Some cat owners around here
should snip a few testicles. If we wise
hominids were sensible, we'd do that too,
or eat our young, like sharks.
But it's love that does us in. Over and over
again, *He shoots, he scores!* and famine
crouches in the bedsheets, ambushing the pulsing
eiderdown, and the windchill factor hits
thirty below, and pollution pours
out of our chimneys to keep us warm.
February, month of despair,
with a skewered heart in the centre.
I think dire thoughts, and lust for French fries
with a splash of vinegar.
Cat, enough of your greedy whining
and your small pink bumhole.
Off my face! You're the life principle,
more or less, so get going
on a little optimism around here.
Get rid of death. Celebrate increase. Make it be spring.

ASPARAGUS

This afternoon a man leans over
the hard rolls and the curled
butter, and tells me everything: two
women love him, he loves them, what
should he do?

The sun
sifts down through the imperceptibly
brownish urban air. I'm going to
suffer for this: turn red, get
blisters or else cancer. I eat
asparagus with my fingers, he
plunges into description.
He's at his wit's end, sewed
up in his own frenzy. He has
breadcrumbs in his beard.
I wonder
if I should let my hair go grey
so my advice will be better.
I could wrinkle up my eyelids,
look wise. I could get a pet lizard.
You're not crazy, I tell him.
Others have done this. Me too.
Messy love is better than none,
I guess. I'm no authority
on sane living.

Which is all true
and no help at all, because
this form of love is like the pain
of childbirth: so intense
it's hard to remember afterwards,
or what kind of screams and grimaces
it pushed you into.

The shrimp arrive on their skewers,
the courtyard trees unroll
their yellowy caterpillars,
pollen powders our shoulders.
He wants them both, he relates
tortures, the coffee
arrives, and altogether I am amazed
at his stupidities.

I sit looking at him
with a sort of wonder,
or is it envy?

Listen, I say to him,
you're very lucky.

RED FOX

The red fox crosses the ice
intent on none of my business.
It's winter and slim pickings.

I stand in the bushy cemetery,
pretending to watch birds,
but really watching the fox
who could care less.
She pauses on the sheer glare
of the pond. She knows I'm there,
sniffs me in the wind at her shoulder.
If I had a gun or dog
or a raw heart, she'd smell it.
She didn't get this smart for nothing.

She's a lean vixen: I can see
the ribs, the sly
trickster's eyes, filled with longing
and desperation, the skinny
feet, adept at lies.

Why encourage the notion
of virtuous poverty?
It's only an excuse
for zero charity.
Hunger corrupts, and absolute hunger
corrupts absolutely,
or almost. Of course there are mothers,
squeezing their breasts
dry, pawning their bodies,
shedding teeth for their children,
or that's our fond belief.
But remember – Hansel
and Gretel were dumped in the forest
because their parents were starving.
Sauve qui peut. To survive
we'd all turn thief

and rascal, or so says the fox,
with her coat of an elegant scoundrel,
her white knife of a smile,
who knows just where she's going:

to steal something
that doesn't belong to her –
some chicken, or one more chance,
or other life.

II

MISS JULY GROWS OLDER

How much longer can I get away
with being so fucking cute?
Not much longer.
The shoes with bows, the cunning underwear
with slogans on the crotch – *Knock Here*,
and so forth –
will have to go, along with the cat suit.
After a while you forget
what you really look like.
You think your mouth is the size it was.
You pretend not to care.

When I was young I went with my hair
hiding one eye, thinking myself daring;
off to the movies in my jaunty pencil
skirt and elastic cinch-belt,
chewed gum, left lipstick
imprints the shape of grateful, rubbery
sighs on the cigarettes of men
I hardly knew and didn't want to.
Men were a skill, you had to have
good hands, breathe into
their nostrils, as for horses. It was something I did well,
like playing the flute, although I don't.

In the forests of grey stems there are standing pools,
tarn-coloured, choked with brown leaves.
Through them you can see an arm, a shoulder,
when the light is right, with the sky clouded.
The train goes past silos, through meadows,
the winter wheat on the fields like scanty fur.

I still get letters, although not many.
A man writes me, requesting true-life stories
about bad sex. He's doing an anthology.
He got my name off an old calendar,
the photo that's mostly bum and daisies,

back when my skin had the golden slick
of fresh-spread margarine.
Not rape, he says, but disappointment,
more like a defeat of expectations.
Dear Sir, I reply, I never had any.
Bad sex, that is.
It was never the sex, it was the other things,
the absence of flowers, the death threats,
the eating habits at breakfast.
I notice I'm using the past tense.

Though the vaporous cloud of chemicals that enveloped
you like a glowing eggshell, an incense,
doesn't disappear: it just gets larger
and takes in more. You grow out
of sex like a shrunk dress
into your common senses, those you share
with whatever's listening. The way the sun
moves through the hours becomes important,
the smeared raindrops
on the window, buds
on the roadside weeds, the sheen
of spilled oil on a raw ditch
filling with muddy water.

Don't get me wrong: with the lights out
I'd still take on anyone,
if I had the energy to spare.
But after a while these flesh arpeggios get boring,
like Bach over and over;
too much of one kind of glory.

When I was all body I was lazy.
I had an easy life, and was not grateful.
Now there are more of me.
Don't confuse me with my hen-leg elbows:
what you get is no longer
what you see.

MANET'S OLYMPIA

She reclines, more or less.
Try that posture, it's hardly languor.
Her right arm sharp angles.
With her left she conceals her ambush.
Shoes but not stockings,
how sinister. The flower
behind her ear is naturally
not real, of a piece
with the sofa's drapery.
The windows (if any) are shut.
This is indoor sin.
Above the head of the (clothed) maid
is an invisible voice balloon: *Slut*.

But. Consider the body,
unfragile, defiant, the pale nipples
staring you right in the bull's-eye.
Consider also the black ribbon
around the neck. What's under it?
A fine red threadline, where the head
was taken off and glued back on.
The body's on offer,
but the neck's as far as it goes.
This is no morsel.
Put clothes on her and you'd have a schoolteacher,
the kind with the brittle whiphand.

There's someone else in this room.
You, Monsieur Voyeur.
As for that object of yours
she's seen those before, and better.

I, the head, am the only subject
of this picture.
You, Sir, are furniture.
Get stuffed.

DAPHNE AND LAURA AND SO FORTH

He was the one who saw me
just before I changed,
before bark/fur/snow closed over
my mouth, before my eyes grew eyes.

I should not have shown fear,
or so much leg.

His look of disbelief –
I didn't mean to!
Just, her neck was so much more
fragile than I thought.

The gods don't listen to reason,
they need what they need –
that suntan line at the bottom
of the spine, those teeth like mouthwash,
that drop of sweat pearling
the upper lip –
or that's what gets said in court.

Why talk when you can whisper?
Rustle, like dried leaves.
Under the bed.

It's ugly here, but safer.
I have eight fingers
and a shell, and live in corners.
I'm free to stay up all night.
I'm working on
these ideas of my own:
venom, a web, a hat,
some last resort.

He was running,
he was asking something,
wanted something or other.

CRESSIDA TO TROILUS: A GIFT

You forced me to give you poisonous gifts.
I can put this no other way.
Everything I gave was to get rid of you
as one gives to a beggar: *There. Go away.*
The first time, the first sentence even
was in answer to your silent clamour
and not for love, and therefore not
a gift, but to get you out of my hair
or whatever part of me you had slid into
by stealth, by creeping up the stairs,

so that whenever I turned, watering
the narcissus, brushing my teeth,
there you were, just barely, in the corner
of my eye. Peripheral. A floater. No one
ever told you greed and hunger
are not the same.

How did all of this start?
With Pity, that flimsy angel,
with her wet pink eyes and slippery wings
of mucous membrane.
She causes so much trouble.

But nothing I ever gave was good for you;
it was like white bread to goldfish.
They cram and cram, and it kills them,
and they drift in the pool, belly-up,
making stunned faces
and playing on our guilt
as if their own toxic gluttony
was not their fault.

There you are still, outside the window,
still with your hands out, still
pallid and fishy-eyed, still acting
stupidly innocent and starved.

Well, take this then. Have some more body.
Drink and eat.
You'll just make yourself sick. Sicker.
You won't be cured.

AVA GARDNER REINCARNATED AS A MAGNOLIA

Somehow I never succeeded
in being taken seriously. They made me
wear things that were ruffled: off-the-
shoulder blouses, the tiered skirts
of flouncing Spanish dancers, though I never
quite got the hauteur – I was always tempted
to wink, show instead of a tragic
outstretched neck, a slice of flank. Now look
at me: a vaginal hot pink,
vibrant as a laxative bottle –
not, given the company, a respectable
colour. Let's face it: when I was in
the flesh, to be beautiful and to be
a woman was a kind
of joke. The men wanted to nail
me in the trophy room, on the pool-
table if possible, the women simply to poke
my eyes out. Me, I would have preferred
to enjoy myself – a little careless
love, some laughs, a few drinks –
but that was not an option.

What would have given
me weight? Substance? For them.
Long canines? Vengeance?
A stiletto hidden in my skirt,
a greyish rainbow of fate
like an aureole of rancid lard –
or better: dress up in armour,
ride across the steppes, leading a horde
of armed murderers. That gets you a statue,
copper or stone, with a lofty frown
– jaw clenched as if chewing –
like those erected by the sober
citizens, years later,
for all the sad destroyers.

Well, to hell with them. I'd rather
be a flower, even this one, so much like
a toilet-paper decoration
at a high-school dance.
Even that, to be trampled
underfoot next day by the janitor
sweeping up, even the damp flirtation,
the crumpled tulle, even the botched smooch
in the parking lot, the boy with the fat neck
and the hip flask, even the awkward fumbling
with the wired bodice, cheap perfume between
the freckled breasts, would have been better
than all their history, the smudged
flags, dry parchments, layers of dead bone
they find so solemn, the slaughters
they like to memorize, and tell
their children also to pray to

here, where they hate bouquets, the pleasures
of thoughtless botany, a glass
of wine or two on the terrace,
bare leg against white trouser
under the table, that ancient ploy
and vital puzzle, water-
of-life cliché that keeps things going,

tawdry and priceless, the breeze
that riffles through what now
may be my leaves, my green closed
eyes, my negligible
vulgar fragile incandescent petals,
these many mouths, lipsticked and showy
and humid as kisses opening
in a hothouse, oh I'd give anything
to have it back again, in
the flesh, the flesh,
which was all the time
I ever had for anything. The joy.

HELEN OF TROY DOES COUNTER DANCING

The world is full of women
who'd tell me I should be ashamed of myself
if they had the chance. Quit dancing.
Get some self-respect
and a day job.
Right. And minimum wage,
and varicose veins, just standing
in one place for eight hours
behind a glass counter
bundled up to the neck, instead of
naked as a meat sandwich.
Selling gloves, or something.
Instead of what I do sell.
You have to have talent
to peddle a thing so nebulous
and without material form.
Exploited, they'd say. Yes, any way
you cut it, but I've a choice
of how, and I'll take the money.

I do give value.
Like preachers, I sell vision,
like perfume ads, desire
or its facsimile. Like jokes
or war, it's all in the timing.
I sell men back their worst suspicions:
that everything's for sale,
and piecemeal. They gaze at me and see
a chain-saw murder just before it happens,
when thigh, ass, inkblot, crevice, tit, and nipple
are still connected.
Such hatred leaps in them,
my beery worshippers! That, or a bleary
hopeless love. Seeing the rows of heads
and upturned eyes, imploring
but ready to snap at my ankles,
I understand floods and earthquakes, and the urge
to step on ants. I keep the beat,
and dance for them because
they can't. The music smells like foxes,
crisp as heated metal
searing the nostrils
or humid as August, hazy and languorous
as a looted city the day after,
when all the rape's been done
already, and the killing,
and the survivors wander around
looking for garbage
to eat, and there's only a bleak exhaustion.

Speaking of which, it's the smiling
tires me out the most.
This, and the pretence
that I can't hear them.
And I can't, because I'm after all
a foreigner to them.
The speech here is all warty gutturals,
obvious as a slab of ham,
but I come from the province of the gods
where meanings are lilting and oblique.

I don't let on to everyone,
but lean close, and I'll whisper:
My mother was raped by a holy swan.
You believe that? You can take me out to dinner.
That's what we tell all the husbands.
There sure are a lot of dangerous birds around.

Not that anyone here
but you would understand.
The rest of them would like to watch me
and feel nothing. Reduce me to components
as in a clock factory or abattoir.
Crush out the mystery.
Wall me up alive
in my own body.
They'd like to see through me,
but nothing is more opaque
than absolute transparency.
Look – my feet don't hit the marble!
Like breath or a balloon, I'm rising,
I hover six inches in the air
in my blazing swan-egg of light.
You think I'm not a goddess?
Try me.
This is a torch song.
Touch me and you'll burn.

A MAN LOOKS

A man looks at a beautiful woman
who is trying to get him through a door,
him and his leg-brace: clumsy hammered
carapace of metal,
shrapnel on the outside of his body
from a war he must have forgotten
or never fought. Some spike

on him is caught down there. She bends over
and he looks at her graceful rump, and thinks *rump*,
and then thinks: *pear on a plate,*
and, on the underside, two apples.
He can't believe he can be so trite,
like some shoddy derivative painter,
and so removed from her. Aren't those thighs?
Isn't that hair? He opens the thighs, strokes the hair,
nothing stirs. He thinks harder, tries *vulva*;
a word like a part in a car motor,
something made of rubber, an oily valve
that squeezes and turns itself inside out.
No hope for it. Once
he would have been able to smell her,
pungency of spring pond and soft onions
mixed with a coy deodorant,
eyelet and armpit, and beyond that
the murmur of willows, leaves
of sunlit weeds crushed under her,
but now she has no such halo.

She stands up and smiles at him,
a smile so translucent
he wrinkles in it, like the skin
on steamed milk.
He's nothing to her but luggage
she needs to haul from room to room,
or a sick dog to be kind to.
She says, 'Shall we try again?'
He thinks, *I am angry.* She takes his arm.
He thinks, *I will die soon.*

SEKHMET, THE LION-HEADED GODDESS OF WAR, VIOLENT STORMS, PESTILENCE, AND RECOVERY FROM ILLNESS, CONTEMPLATES THE DESERT IN THE METROPOLITAN MUSEUM OF ART

He was the sort of man
who wouldn't hurt a fly.
Many flies are now alive
while he is not.
He was not my patron.
He preferred full granaries, I battle.
My roar meant slaughter.
Yet here we are together
in the same museum.
That's not what I see, though, the fitful
crowds of staring children
learning the lesson of multi-
cultural obliteration, *sic transit*
and so on.

I see the temple where I was born
or built, where I held power.
I see the desert beyond,
where the hot conical tombs, that look
from a distance, frankly, like dunces' hats,
hide my jokes: the dried-out flesh
and bones, the wooden boats
in which the dead sail endlessly
in no direction.

What did you expect from gods
with animal heads?
Though come to think of it
the ones made later, who were fully human,
were not such good news either.
Favour me and give me riches,
destroy my enemies.
That seems to be the gist.
Oh yes: *And save me from death.*
In return we're given blood
and bread, flowers and prayer,
and lip service.

Maybe there's something in all of this
I missed. But if it's selfless
love you're looking for,
you've got the wrong goddess.

I just sit where I'm put, composed
of stone and wishful thinking:
that the deity who kills for pleasure
will also heal,
that in the midst of your nightmare,
the final one, a kind lion
will come with bandages in her mouth
and the soft body of a woman,
and lick you clean of fever,
and pick your soul up gently by the nape of the neck
and caress you into darkness and paradise.

III

ROMANTIC

Men and their mournful romanticisms
that can't get the dishes done –
that's freedom, that broken wineglass
in the cold fireplace.

When women wash underpants, it's a chore.
When men do it, an intriguing affliction.
How plangent, the damp socks flapping on the line,
how lost and single in the orphaning air . . .

She cherishes that sadness,
tells him to lie down on the grass,
closes each of his eyes with a finger,
applies her body like a poultice.

You poor thing, said the Australian woman
while he held our baby –
as if I had forced him to do it,
as if I had my high heel in his face.

Still, who's taken in?
Every time?
Us, and our empty hands, the hands
of starving nurses.

It's bullet holes we want to see in their skin,
scars, and the chance to touch them.

CELL

Now look objectively. You have to
admit the cancer cell is beautiful.
If it were a flower, you'd say, *How pretty*,
with its mauve centre and pink petals

or if a cover for a pulpy thirties
sci-fi magazine, *How striking*;
as an alien, a success,
all purple eye and jelly tentacles
and spines, or are they gills,
creeping around on granular Martian
dirt red as the inside of the body,

while its tender walls
expand and burst, its spores
scatter elsewhere, take root, like money,
drifting like a fiction or
miasma in and out of people's
brains, digging themselves
industriously in. The lab technician

says, *It has forgotten*
how to die. But why remember? All it wants is more
amnesia. More life, and more abundantly. To take
more. To eat more. To replicate itself. To keep on
doing those things forever. Such desires
are not unknown. Look in the mirror.

THE LONELINESS OF THE MILITARY HISTORIAN

Confess: it's my profession
that alarms you.
This is why few people ask me to dinner,
though Lord knows I don't go out of my way to be scary.
I wear dresses of sensible cut
and unalarming shades of beige,
I smell of lavender and go to the hairdresser's:
no prophetess mane of mine,
complete with snakes, will frighten the youngsters.
If I roll my eyes and mutter,
if I clutch at my heart and scream in horror
like a third-rate actress chewing up a mad scene,
I do it in private and nobody sees
but the bathroom mirror.

In general I might agree with you:
women should not contemplate war,
should not weigh tactics impartially,
or evade the word *enemy*,
or view both sides and denounce nothing.
Women should march for peace,
or hand out white feathers to arouse bravery,
spit themselves on bayonets
to protect their babies,
whose skulls will be split anyway,
or, having been raped repeatedly,
hang themselves with their own hair.
These are the functions that inspire general comfort.
That, and the knitting of socks for the troops
and a sort of moral cheerleading.
Also: mourning the dead.
Sons, lovers, and so forth.
All the killed children.

Instead of this, I tell
what I hope will pass as truth.
A blunt thing, not lovely.

The truth is seldom welcome,
especially at dinner,
though I am good at what I do.
My trade is courage and atrocities.
I look at them and do not condemn.
I write things down the way they happened,
as near as can be remembered.
I don't ask *why*, because it is mostly the same.
Wars happen because the ones who start them
think they can win.

In my dreams there is glamour.
The Vikings leave their fields
each year for a few months of killing and plunder,
much as the boys go hunting.
In real life they were farmers.
They come back loaded with splendour.
The Arabs ride against Crusaders
with scimitars that could sever
silk in the air.
A swift cut to the horse's neck
and a hunk of armour crashes down
like a tower. Fire against metal.
A poet might say: romance against banality.
When awake, I know better.

Despite the propaganda, there are no monsters,
or none that can be finally buried.
Finish one off and circumstances
and the radio create another.
Believe me: whole armies have prayed fervently
to God all night and meant it,
and been slaughtered anyway.
Brutality wins frequently,
and large outcomes have turned on the invention
of a mechanical device, viz. radar.
True, valour sometimes counts for something,
as at Thermopylae. Sometimes being right –
though ultimate virtue, by agreed tradition,
is decided by the winner.

Sometimes men throw themselves on grenades
and burst like paper bags of guts
to save their comrades.
I can admire that.
But rats and cholera have won many wars.
Those, and potatoes,
or the absence of them.
It's no use pinning all those medals
across the chests of the dead.
Impressive, but I know too much.
Grand exploits merely depress me.

In the interests of research
I have walked on many battlefields
that once were liquid with pulped
men's bodies and spangled with exploded
shells and splayed bone.
All of them have been green again
by the time I got there.
Each has inspired a few good quotes in its day.
Sad marble angels brood like hens
over the grassy nests where nothing hatches.
(The angels could just as well be described as *vulgar*
or *pitiless*, depending on camera angle.)
The word *glory* figures a lot on gateways.
Of course I pick a flower or two
from each, and press it in the hotel Bible
for a souvenir.
I'm just as human as you.

But it's no use asking me for a final statement.
As I say, I deal in tactics.
Also statistics:
for every year of peace there have been four hundred
years of war.

MARSH LANGUAGES

The dark soft languages are being silenced:
Mothertongue   Mothertongue   Mothertongue
falling one by one back into the moon.

Language of marshes,
language of the roots of rushes tangled
together in the ooze,
marrow cells twinning themselves
inside the warm core of the bone:
pathways of hidden light in the body fade and wink out.

The sibilants and gutturals,
the cave language, the half-light
forming at the back of the throat,
the mouth's damp velvet moulding
the lost syllable for 'I' that did not mean separate,
all are becoming sounds no longer
heard because no longer spoken,
and everything that could once be said in them has
  ceased to exist.

The languages of the dying suns
are themselves dying,
but even the word for this has been forgotten.
The mouth against skin, vivid and fading,
can no longer speak both cherishing and farewell.
It is now only a mouth, only skin.
There is no more longing.

Translation was never possible.
Instead there was always only
conquest, the influx
of the language of hard nouns,
the language of metal,
the language of either/or,
the one language that has eaten all the others.

FROGLESS

The sore trees cast their leaves
too early. Each twig pinching
shut like a jabbed clam.
Soon there will be a hot gauze of snow
searing the roots.

Booze in the spring runoff,
pure antifreeze;
the stream worms drunk and burning.
Tadpoles wrecked in the puddles.

Here comes an eel with a dead eye
grown from its cheek.
Would you cook it?
You would if.

The people eat sick fish
because there are no others.
Then they get born wrong.

This is not sport, sir.
This is not good weather.
This is not blue and green.

This is home.
Travel anywhere in a year, five years,
and you'll end up here.

HALF-HANGED MARY

('Half-hanged Mary' was Mary Webster, who was accused of witchcraft in the 1680s in a Puritan town in Massachusetts and hanged from a tree – where, according to one of the several surviving accounts, she was left all night. It is known that when she was cut down she was still alive, since she lived for another fourteen years.)

7 p.m.

Rumour was loose in the air,
hunting for some neck to land on.
I was milking the cow,
the barn door open to the sunset.

I didn't feel the aimed word hit
and go in like a soft bullet.
I didn't feel the smashed flesh
closing over it like water
over a thrown stone.

I was hanged for living alone,
for having blue eyes and a sunburned skin,
tattered skirts, few buttons,
a weedy farm in my own name,
and a surefire cure for warts;

Oh yes, and breasts,
and a sweet pear hidden in my body.
Whenever there's talk of demons
these come in handy.

8 p.m.

The rope was an improvisation.
With time they'd have thought of axes.

Up I go like a windfall in reverse,
a blackened apple stuck back onto the tree.

Trussed hands, rag in my mouth,
a flag raised to salute the moon,

old bone-faced goddess, old original,
who once took blood in return for food.

The men of the town stalk homeward,
excited by their show of hate,

their own evil turned inside out like a glove,
and me wearing it.

9 p.m.

The bonnets come to stare,
the dark skirts also,
the upturned faces in between,
mouths closed so tight they're lipless.
I can see down into their eyeholes
and nostrils. I can see their fear.

You were my friend, you too.
I cured your baby, Mrs.,
and flushed yours out of you,
Non-wife, to save your life.

Help me down? You don't dare.
I might rub off on you,
like soot or gossip. Birds
of a feather burn together,
though as a rule ravens are singular.

In a gathering like this one
the safe place is the background,
pretending you can't dance,
the safe stance pointing a finger.

I understand. You can't spare
anything, a hand, a piece of bread, a shawl
against the cold,
a good word. Lord
knows there isn't much
to go around. You need it all.

10 p.m.

Well God, now that I'm up here
with maybe some time to kill
away from the daily
fingerwork, legwork, work
at the hen level,
we can continue our quarrel,
the one about free will.

Is it my choice that I'm dangling
like a turkey's wattles from this
more than indifferent tree?
If Nature is Your alphabet,
what letter is this rope?

Does my twisting body spell out Grace?
I hurt, therefore I am.
Faith, Charity, and Hope
are three dead angels
falling like meteors or
burning owls across
the profound blank sky of Your face.

12 midnight

My throat is taut against the rope
choking off words and air;
I'm reduced to knotted muscle.
Blood bulges in my skull,
my clenched teeth hold it in;
I bite down on despair.

Death sits on my shoulder like a crow
waiting for my squeezed beet
of a heart to burst
so he can eat my eyes

or like a judge
muttering about sluts and punishment
and licking his lips

or like a dark angel
insidious in his glossy feathers
whispering to me to be easy
on myself. To breathe out finally.
Trust me, he says, caressing
me. *Why suffer?*

A temptation, to sink down
into these definitions.
To become a martyr in reverse,
or food, or trash.

To give up my own words for myself,
my own refusals.
To give up knowing.
To give up pain.
To let go.

2 a.m.

Out of my mouth is coming, at some
distance from me, a thin gnawing sound
which you could confuse with prayer except that
praying is not constrained.

Or is it, Lord?
Maybe it's more like being strangled
than I once thought. Maybe it's
a gasp for air, prayer.
Did those men at Pentecost
want flames to shoot out of their heads?
Did they ask to be tossed
on the ground, gabbling like holy poultry,
eyeballs bulging?

As mine are, as mine are.
There is only one prayer; it is not
the knees in the clean nightgown
on the hooked rug,
I want this, I want that.
Oh far beyond.
Call it *Please*. Call it *Mercy*.
Call it *Not yet, not yet,*
as Heaven threatens to explode
inwards in fire and shredded flesh, and the angels caw.

3 a.m.

wind seethes in the leaves around
me the trees exude night
birds night birds yell inside
my ears like stabbed hearts my heart
stutters in my fluttering cloth
body I dangle with strength
going out of me the wind seethes
in my body tattering
the words I clench
my fists hold No
talisman or silver disc my lungs
flail as if drowning I call
on you as witness I did
no crime I was born I have borne I
bear I will be born this is
a crime I will not
acknowledge leaves and wind
hold on to me
I will not give in

6 a.m.

Sun comes up, huge and blaring,
no longer a simile for God.
Wrong address. I've been out there.

Time is relative, let me tell you
I have lived a millennium.

I would like to say my hair turned white
overnight, but it didn't.
Instead it was my heart:
bleached out like meat in water.

Also, I'm about three inches taller.
This is what happens when you drift in space

listening to the gospel
of the red-hot stars.
Pinpoints of infinity riddle my brain,
a revelation of deafness.

At the end of my rope
I testify to silence.
Don't say I'm not grateful.

Most will have only one death.
I will have two.

8 a.m.

When they came to harvest my corpse
(open your mouth, close your eyes)
cut my body from the rope,
surprise, surprise:
I was still alive.

Tough luck, folks,
I know the law:
you can't execute me twice
for the same thing. How nice.

I fell to the clover, breathed it in,
and bared my teeth at them
in a filthy grin.
You can imagine how that went over.

Now I only need to look
out at them through my sky-blue eyes.
They see their own ill will
staring them in the forehead
and turn tail.

Before, I was not a witch.
But now I am one.

Later

My body of skin waxes and wanes
around my true body,
a tender nimbus.
I skitter over the paths and fields
mumbling to myself like crazy,
mouth full of juicy adjectives
and purple berries.
The townsfolk dive headfirst into the bushes
to get out of my way.

My first death orbits my head,
an ambiguous nimbus,
medallion of my ordeal.
No one crosses that circle.

Having been hanged for something
I never said,
I can now say anything I can say.

Holiness gleams on my dirty fingers,
I eat flowers and dung,
two forms of the same thing, I eat mice
and give thanks, blasphemies
gleam and burst in my wake
like lovely bubbles.
I speak in tongues,
my audience is owls.

My audience is God,
because who the hell else could understand me?
Who else has been dead twice?

The words boil out of me,
coil after coil of sinuous possibility.
The cosmos unravels from my mouth,
all fullness, all vacancy.

OWL BURNING

A few inches down and the soil stops
like a bolted door. A hard frost and that's that
for anything left unharvested.

Why should an old woman suck up the space,
the black roots, red juice that should be going
instead into the children?

Of course she practised magic.
When you're that hungry
you need such hooks and talons.

Held her breath at midnight, uncrossed her fingers,
and owls' feathers sprouted all over her
like mould on meat, but faster.

Saw her myself, hunting mice
in the moonlight. Silent
as the shadow of a hand thrown by a candle.

A good disguise, but I knew it was her
next day, by the white feather
caught in her hair.

She burned extremely, thick fat on fire.
Making grey screams. Giving back
to the air what she took when she shrivelled us.

She might have saved herself
with her white owl's voice
but we cut parts off her first

so she couldn't fly.
The fingers, those are the wings.
We watched her smoulder and got drunk after.

Her heart was the ember
we used to relight our stoves.
This is our culture,

no business of yours.
You have soft feet.
You don't know what it's like,
so close to bedrock.

DOWN

i.

They were wrong about the sun.
It does not go down into
the underworld at night.
The sun leaves merely
and the underworld emerges.
It can happen at any moment.

It can happen in the morning,
you in the kitchen going through
your mild routines.
Plate, cup, knife.
All at once there's no blue, no green,
no warning.

ii.

Old thread, old line
of ink twisting out into the clearness
we call space
where are you leading me this time?

Past the stove, past the table,
past the daily horizontal
of the floor, past the cellar,
past the believable,
down into the darkness
where you reverse and shine.

iii.

At first you think they are angels,
these albino voices, these voices
like the unpainted eyes of statues,
these mute voices like gloves
with no hands in them,
these moth voices fluttering
and baffled around your ears,
trying to make you hear them.

What do they need?

You make a cut in yourself,
a little opening
for the pain to get in.
You set loose three drops of your blood.

iv.

This is
the kingdom of the unspoken,
the kingdom of the unspeaking:

all those destroyed by war
all those who are starving
all those beaten to death
and buried in pits, those slit apart
for reasons of expediency or money
all those howling
in locked rooms, all sacrificed
children, all murdered brides,
all suicides.

They say:
Speak for us (to whom)
Some say: *Avenge us* (on whom)
Some say: *Take our place.*
Some say: *Witness.*

Others say (and these are women):
Be happy for us.

v.

There is the staircase,
there is the sun.
There is the kitchen,
the plate with toast and strawberry jam,
your subterfuge,
your ordinary mirage.

You stand red-handed.
You want to wash yourself
in earth, in rocks and grass

What are you supposed to do
with all this loss?

A PINK HOTEL IN CALIFORNIA

My father chops with his axe
and the leaves fall off the trees.
It's nineteen forty-three.
He's splitting wood for the winter.
His gun leans behind the door,
beside his goose-greased workboots.
Smoke comes out of the metal chimney.

At night I sleep in a bunk bed.
The waves stroke the lake.
In the mornings it is so cold
we can see our breath
and the ice on the rocky shore.
My mother rakes the ashes
out from under the oven.

This is comfort and safety,
the sound of chopping in the empty forest,
the smell of smoke.
It's nineteen forty-three.
After it rains we have a bonfire.
The children dance around it,
singing about the war
which is happening elsewhere.
What has become of them, those words
that once shone with such
glossy innocence?
I rolled them in my mouth like marbles,
they tasted pure:
smoke, gun, boots, oven.
The fire. The scattered ashes. The winter forest.

I sit in a pink room;
the chest of drawers
has antique man-bored wormholes.
Isn't there enough of the past
without making more?

It's nineteen forty-three.
It's nineteen ninety-four,
I can hear the sound of the chopping.
It's because of the ocean,
it's because of the war
which won't stay under the waves and leaves.
The carpet smells of ashes.

This is the pink hotel
where everything recurs
and nothing is elsewhere.

IV

MAN IN A GLACIER

Now see: they've found a man in a glacier,
two thousand years old, or three,
with everything intact: shoes, teeth, and arrows,
closed eyes, fur hat, the charm he wore to protect him
from death by snow. They think he must have been
a messenger, done in by bad weather,
and still fresh as a mastodon. Then there's

the box of slides in the cellar
my brother found, the kind we used to
tape between glass. As it turns out
the wrong thing for mildew.
Some cleaning, scraping away those little
flowers of crystallizing earth, and then
a wand of light, and here's my father,
alive or else preserved, younger than all
of us now, dark-haired and skinny,
in baggy trousers, woollen legs tucked into
those lace-up boots of our ancestors,
by a lake, feeding a picnic fire
in the clear blue-tinged air of either
a northern summer or else a film
of ageing gelatin spread thinly
with fading colours,
the reds pushing towards pink, the greens greying,

but there. There still. This was all we got,
this echo, this freeze-framed
simulacrum or slight imprint,
in answer to our prayers for everlastingness,

the first time we discovered
we could not stop, or live backwards;
when we opened
our eyes, found we were rocked

with neither love nor malice in the ruthless
icy arms of Chemistry and Physics, our
bad godmothers. It was they
who were present at our birth, who laid
the curse on us: *You will not sleep forever.*

WAVE

He was sitting in a chair at dinner
and a wave washed over him.
Suddenly, whole beaches
were simply gone.
1947. Lake Superior. Last year.

But the cabin, I said, that one,
the one with the owl –
don't you remember?
Nothing was left. No feathers.

We remained to him in fragments.
Why are you so old, he asked me,
all of a sudden?
Where is this forest? Why am I so cold?
Please take me home.

Outside, the neighbour mowed the lawn.
It's all right here, I said.
There are no bears.
There's food. It isn't snowing.

No. We need more wood, he said.
The winter's on its way.
It will be bad.

KING LEAR IN RESPITE CARE

The daughters have their parties.
Who can cope?
He's left here in a chair
he can't get out of
in all this snow, or possibly
wallpaper. Wheeled somewhere.
He will have to be sly and stubborn
and not let on.

Another man's hand
coming out of a tweed sleeve that isn't
his, curls on his knee. He can move it with the other
hand. Howling would be uncalled for.

Who knows what he knows?
Many things, but where he is
isn't among them. How did it happen,
this cave, this hovel?
It may or may not be noon.

Time is another element
you never think about
until it's gone.
Things like ceilings, or air.

Someone comes to brush
his hair, wheel him to tea-time.
Old women gather around
in pearls and florals. They want to flirt.
An old man is so rare.
He's a hero just by being here.

They giggle. They disappear
behind the hawthorn bushes
in bloom, or possibly sofas.
Now he's been left alone
with the television turned on
to the weather programme, the sound down.

The cold blast sweeps across
the waste field of the afternoon.
Rage occurs,
followed by supper:
something he can't taste,
a brownish texture.

The sun goes down. The trees bend,
they straighten up. They bend.

At eight the youngest daughter comes.
She holds his hand.
She says, *Did they feed you?*
He says no.
He says, *Get me out of here.*
He wants so much to say *please*,
but won't.

After a pause, she says –
he hears her say –
I love you like salt.

A VISIT

Gone are the days
when you could walk on water.
When you could walk.

The days are gone.
Only one day remains,
the one you're in.

The memory is no friend.
It can only tell you
what you no longer have:

a left hand you can use,
two feet that walk.
All the brain's gadgets.

Hello, hello.
The one hand that still works
grips, won't let go.

That is not a train.
There is no cricket.
Let's not panic.

Let's talk about axes,
which kinds are good,
the many names of wood.

This is how to build
a house, a boat, a tent.
No use; the toolbox

refuses to reveal its verbs;
the rasp, the plane, the awl
revert to sullen metal.

Do you recognize anything? I said.
Anything familiar?
Yes, you said. The bed.

Better to watch the stream
that flows across the floor
and is made of sunlight,

the forest made of shadows;
better to watch the fireplace
which is now a beach.

DANCING

It was my father taught my mother
how to dance.
I never knew that.
I thought it was the other way.
Ballroom was their style,
a graceful twirling,
curved arms and fancy footwork,
a green-eyed radio.

There is always more than you know.
There are always boxes
put away in the cellar,
worn shoes and cherished pictures,
notes you find later,
sheet music you can't play.

A woman came on Wednesdays
with tapes of waltzes.
She tried to make him shuffle
around the floor with her.
She said it would be good for him.
He didn't want to.

BORED

All those times I was bored
out of my mind. Holding the log
while he sawed it. Holding
the string while he measured, boards,
distances between things, or pounded
stakes into the ground for rows and rows
of lettuces and beets, which I then (bored)
weeded. Or sat in the back
of the car, or sat still in boats,
sat, sat, while at the prow, stern, wheel
he drove, steered, paddled. It
wasn't even boredom, it was looking,
looking hard and up close at the small
details. Myopia. The worn gunwales,
the intricate twill of the seat
cover. The acid crumbs of loam, the granular
pink rock, its igneous veins, the sea-fans
of dry moss, the blackish and then the greying
bristles on the back of his neck.
Sometimes he would whistle, sometimes
I would. The boring rhythm of doing
things over and over, carrying
the wood, drying
the dishes. Such minutiae. It's what
the animals spend most of their time at,
ferrying the sand, grain by grain, from their tunnels,
shuffling the leaves in their burrows. He pointed
such things out, and I would look
at the whorled texture of his square finger, earth under
the nail. Why do I remember it as sunnier
all the time then, although it more often
rained, and more birdsong?
I could hardly wait to get
the hell out of there to
anywhere else. Perhaps though
boredom is happier. It is for dogs or

groundhogs. Now I wouldn't be bored.
Now I would know too much.
Now I would know.

FLOWERS

Right now I am the flower girl.
I bring fresh flowers,
dump out the old ones, the greenish water
that smells like dirty teeth
into the bathroom sink, snip off the stem ends
with surgical scissors I borrowed
from the nursing station,
put them into a jar
I brought from home, because they don't have vases
in this hotel for the ill,
place them on the table beside my father
where he can't see them
because he won't open his eyes.

He lies flattened under the white sheet.
He says he is on a ship,
and I can see it –
the functional white walls, the minimal windows,
the little bells, the rubbery footsteps of strangers,
the whispering all around
of the air-conditioner, or else the ocean,

and he is on a ship;
he's giving us up, giving up everything
but the breath going in
and out of his diminished body;
minute by minute he's sailing slowly away,
away from us and our waving hands
that do not wave.

The women come in, two of them, in blue;
it's no use being kind, in here,
if you don't have hands like theirs –
large and capable, the hands
of plump muscular angels,
the ones that blow trumpets and lift swords.
They shift him carefully, tuck in the corners.
It hurts, but as little as possible.
Pain is their lore. The rest of us
are helpless amateurs.

A suffering you can neither cure nor enter –
there are worse things, but not many.
After a while it makes us impatient.
Can't we do anything but feel sorry?

I sit there, watching the flowers
in their pickle jar. He is asleep, or not.
I think: He looks like a turtle.
Or: He looks erased.
But somewhere in there, at the far end of the tunnel
of pain and forgetting he's trapped in
is the same father I knew before,
the one who carried the green canoe
over the portage, the painter trailing,
myself with the fishing rods, slipping
on the wet boulders and slapping flies.
That was the last time we went there.

There will be a last time for this also,
bringing cut flowers to this white room.
Sooner or later I too
will have to give everything up,
even the sorrow that comes with these flowers,
even the anger,
even the memory of how I brought them
from a garden I will no longer have by then,
and put them beside my dying father,
hoping I could still save him.

TWO DREAMS

In the seven days before his death
I dreamed my father twice.
First by the shore,
the beach, the rocks, the driftwood stumps,
my mother in a blue bathrobe, frantic:
He went into the lake, in all his clothes,
just waded out and sank.
Why did he do that?

I dove to find him –
the shells of crayfish, clam tracks on sand,
drowned stones with their bloom of algae –
but he was too far down.
He still had his hat on.

The second time it was autumn,
we were up on the hill, all the leaves fallen,
by the small cabin that burned down,
each window zinced with frost,
each log restored,
not blurred or faded by dream,
but exact, the way they were.

Such dreams are relentless.

My father is standing there
with his back turned to us
in his winter parka, the hood up.
He never had one like that.

Now he's walking away.
The bright leaves rustle, we can't call,
he doesn't look.

THE TIME

You'd better come down, my brother said.
It's the time. I know death when I see it.
There's a clear look.

The sweet, dire smell of hospitals,
stale piss and disinfectant,
and baby powder.

The nurse said, Has anyone
been away? I said, Me.
Ah, she said. They wait. It's often like that.

My sister said, I was holding
his hand. He winced
like pulling off a bandage,

he frowned. My mother said,
I need some time
with him. Not very long. Alone.

TWO DREAMS, 2

Sitting at noon over the carrot salad
my sister and I compare dreams.

She says, Father was there
in some kind of very strange nightgown
covered with bristles, like a hair shirt.
He was blind, he was stumbling around
bumping into things, and I couldn't stop crying.

I say, Mine was close.
He was still alive, and all of it
was a mistake, but it was our fault.
He couldn't talk, but it was clear
he wanted everything back, the shoes, the binoculars
we'd given away or thrown out.
He was wearing stripes, like a prisoner.
We were trying to be cheerful,
but I wasn't happy to see him:
now we would have to do the whole thing over again.

Who sends us these messages,
oblique and muffled?
What good can they do?

In the daylight we know
what's gone is gone,
but at night it's different.
Nothing gets finished,
not dying, not mourning;
the dead repeat themselves, like clumsy drunks
lurching sideways through the doors
we open to them in sleep;
these slurred guests, never entirely welcome,
even those we have loved the most,
especially those we have loved the most,
returning from where we shoved them
away too quickly:
from under the ground, from under the water,
they clutch at us, they clutch at us,
we won't let go.

OH

It's Christmas, and the green wreaths,
festive and prickly, with their bright red
holly berries, dot the graves,

the shocked mouths grief has made
and keeps on making:
round silent Ohs,
leafy and still alive
that hurt when you touch them.

Look, they are everywhere: Oh. Oh. Oh. Oh.
What else can be said?

Strange how we decorate pain.
These ribbons, for instance,
and the small hard teardrops of blood.
Who are they for?
Do we think the dead care?

It's so cold today
even the birds, those flurries
of light and fever,
freeze in the air.

The bare trees crack overhead
as we place our flowers
already stiff with ice.

In the spring the flowers will melt,
also the berries,
and something will come to eat them.
We will go around
in these circles for a time,
winter summer winter,
and, after more time, not.

This is a good thought.

THE OTTAWA RIVER BY NIGHT

In the full moon you dream more.
I know where I am: the Ottawa River
far up, where the dam goes across.
Once, midstorm, in the wide cold water
upstream, two long canoes full
of children tipped, and they all held hands
and sang till the chill reached their hearts.
I suppose in our waking lives that's the best
we can hope for, if you think of that moment
stretched out for years.
                    Once, my father
and I paddled seven miles
along a lake near here
at night, with the trees like a pelt of dark
hackles, and the waves hardly moving.
In the moonlight the way ahead was clear
and obscure both. I was twenty
and impatient to get there, thinking
such a thing existed.
                    None of this
is in the dream, of course. Just the thick square-
edged shape of the dam, and eastward
the hills of sawdust from the mill, gleaming as white
as dunes. To the left, stillness; to the right,
the swirling foam of rapids
over sharp rocks and snags; and below that, my father,
moving away downstream
in his boat, so skilfully
although dead, I remember now; but no longer as old.
He wears his grey hat, and evidently
he can see again. There now,
he's around the corner. He's heading eventually
to the sea. Not the real one, with its sick whales
and oil slicks, but the other sea, where there can still be
safe arrivals.
          Only a dream, I think, waking
to the sound of nothing.

Not nothing. I heard: it was a beach, or shore,
and someone far off, walking.
Nowhere familiar. Somewhere I've been before.
It always takes a long time
to decipher where you are.

V

VERMILION FLYCATCHER,
SAN PEDRO RIVER, ARIZONA

The river's been here, violent, right where we're standing,
you can tell by the trash caught overhead in the trees.
Now it's a trickle, and we're up to our knees
in late-spring yellowing weeds. A vermilion
flycatcher darts down, flutters up, perches.
Stick a pin in your thumb, the bead of blood
would be his colour. He's filled with joy
and the tranced rage of sex. How he conjures,
with his cry like a needle. A punctuation. A bone button

on fire. Everything bad you can imagine
is happening somewhere else, or happened
here, a hundred years or centuries
ago. He sings, and there's the murder:
you see it, forming under
the shimmering air, a man with brown
or white skin lying reversed
in the vanished water, a spear
or bullet in his back. At the ford, where the deer
come at dusk to cross and drink
and be ambushed. The red bird

is sitting on the same tree, intensely
bright in the sun that gleams on cruelty, on broken
skullbone, arrow, spur. Vultures cluster,
he doesn't care. He and his other-coloured mate
ignore everything but their own rapture.
Who knows what they remember?
Birds never dream, being their own.
Dreams, I mean. As for you, the river
that isn't there is the same one
you could drown in, face down.

THE MOMENT

The moment when, after many years
of hard work and a long voyage
you stand in the centre of your room,
house, half-acre, square mile, island, country,
knowing at last how you got there,
and say, *I own this*,

is the same moment the trees unloose
their soft arms from around you,
the birds take back their language,
the cliffs fissure and collapse,
the air moves back from you like a wave
and you can't breathe.

No, they whisper. *You own nothing.*
You were a visitor, time after time
climbing the hill, planting the flag, proclaiming.
We never belonged to you.
You never found us.
It was always the other way round.

UP

You wake up filled with dread.
There seems no reason for it.
Morning light sifts through the window,
there is birdsong,
you can't get out of bed.

It's something about the crumpled sheets
hanging over the edge like jungle
foliage, the terry slippers gaping
their dark pink mouths for your feet,
the unseen breakfast – some of it
in the refrigerator you do not dare
to open – you will not dare to eat.

What prevents you? The future. The future tense,
immense as outer space.
You could get lost there.
No. Nothing so simple. The past, its density
and drowned events pressing you down,
like sea water, like gelatin
filling your lungs instead of air.

Forget all that and let's get up.
Try moving your arm.
Try moving your head.
Pretend the house is on fire
and you must run or burn.
No, that one's useless.
It's never worked before.

Where is it coming from, this echo,
this huge No that surrounds you,
silent as the folds of the yellow
curtains, mute as the cheerful

Mexican bowl with its cargo
of mummified flowers?
(You chose the colours of the sun,
not the dried neutrals of shadow.
God knows you've tried.)

Now here's a good one:
you're lying on your deathbed.
You have one hour to live.
Who is it, exactly, you have needed
all these years to forgive?

GIRL WITHOUT HANDS

Walking through the ruins
on your way to work
that do not look like ruins
with the sunlight pouring over
the seen world
like hail or melted
silver, that bright
and magnificent, each leaf
and stone quickened and specific in it,
and you can't hold it,
you can't hold any of it. Distance surrounds you,
marked out by the ends of your arms
when they are stretched to their fullest.
You can go no farther than this,
you think, walking forward,
pushing the distance in front of you
like a metal cart on wheels
with its barriers and horizontals.
Appearance melts away from you,
the offices and pyramids
on the horizon shimmer and cease.
No one can enter that circle
you have made, that clean circle
of dead space you have made
and stay inside,
mourning because it is clean.

Then there's the girl, in the white dress,
meaning purity, or the failure
to be any colour. She has no hands, it's true.
The scream that happened to the air
when they were taken off
surrounds her now like an aureole
of hot sand, of no sound.
Everything has bled out of her.

Only a girl like this
can know what's happened to you.
If she were here she would
reach out her arms towards
you now, and touch you
with her absent hands
and you would feel nothing, but you would be
touched all the same.

THE SIGNER

In city after city
in an area of darkness behind my head
stands a woman dressed in black,
even the stockings: my unknown twin.

Only her hands are moving:
they catch the light and throw it
into the silence,
which for some here is total.

In her hands, deft as a knitter's
but quicker, my words turn solid,
become a gesture, a skein,
a semaphore of the body
for those who listen with their eyes.

Unable to see her, I speak
in a kind of blindness, not knowing
what dance is being made of me,

what puns of the thumb, tough
similes of the fingers,
how I translate into bone.

(Yet it is not a translation
you built here, mute sister,

left-handed shadow cast by an absence
that moves you nevertheless to love:

together we are practising
for the place where all the languages
will be finalized and
one; and the hands also.)

A FIRE PLACE

Here is the place where the lightning fire one time
almost got us. Where the heroic youngish
(now dead) men in their chequered flannel
shirts with the sleeves rolled up and their high-laced
lumberjacks' (obsolete) boots once fought it
with hand-pumps and axes to a damp and acrid
standstill. Where the charred trunks lay smouldering.
The whole thing a gash (they said) in the forest. A scar.
Where then poplar seeped in and over, feeding on ashes,
and (purple)
fireweed, and (blue) berries, and the bears, and us
with our lard pails and tin cups, our jelly
sandwiches at lunchtime, skinning our knees on the sooty
rocks, smudging our hands
and mouths with black and blue, in our summer clothing (since
torn into dustcloths, thrown out and rotted away).
Now that bright random clearing
or burn, or meadow if you like, is gone
also, and there's scrubland, a light-green
sticky new forest. Earth does such things
to itself: furrowing, cracking apart, bursting
into flame. It rips openings in itself, which it struggles
(or not) to skin over. The moon
doesn't care about its own
craters and bruises. Only we can regret
the perishing of the burned place.
Only we could call it a wound.

STATUARY

Wingtips, fingertips, nipples, and penises –
the parts we once flew with are broken
away first by whoever it is with a hammer,
to whom the body's flights are an affront.
Who are you, you who shamble and roll
like an unseen boulder or troll through parks and cemeteries
and wish to keep us earthbound?
After that the noses go, and then
the toes, if any. You want to keep us from walking,
however heavily, on our limestone feet
in search of our lost trajectories.
Then our arms. Enfolding is taken from us,
and clasp. Our mouths erode in the rain
you send, and all our bright definite
nouns and quick verbs with them.
We are ground down to our torsos,
just those, and our heads, increasingly
blunted and smoothed of gesture,
each of us a vestigial stump
topped with a doorknob. Then
headless, a stub, like a whale's tooth or a tongue
cut out of a face and frozen.

Even this isn't enough for you.
You won't be content until we're toppled,
like you, by frost-heave or vandals, and lie melting
in the uncut grass, like you. In the tall weeds. In the young trees.
Until we're rubble. Like you. Until we're pebbles
on the shore of a vast lake that doesn't (like you) exist yet.
Until we're liquid, like you; like the small whirlpools
an oar makes drawn slowly through water,

those darkly shining swirls the shape of a galaxy,
those knotholes the world turns itself inside out through
for us, for a moment, the nothingness
that by its moving
edges defines time. That lets us see down
and into. That lets us fly
and embody, like you. Until we are like you.

SHAPECHANGERS IN WINTER

I.

Through the slit of our open window, the wind
comes in and flows around us, nothingness
in motion, like time. The power of what is not there.
The snow empties itself down, a shadow turning
to indigo, obliterating
everything out there, roofs, cars, garbage cans,
dead flowerstalks, dog turds, it doesn't matter.
You could read this as indifference
on the part of the universe, or else a relentless
forgiveness: all of our
scratches and blots and mortal
wounds and patched-up jobs
wiped clean in the snow's huge erasure.

I feel it as a pressure,
an added layer:
above, the white waterfall of snow
thundering down; then attic, moth-balled
sweaters, nomadic tents,
the dried words of old letters;
then stairs, then children, cats and radiators, peeling paint,
us in our bed, the afterglow
of a smoky fire, our one candle flickering;
below us, the kitchen in the dark, the wink
of pots on shelves; then books and tools, then cellar
and furnace, greying dolls, a bicycle,
the whole precarious geology of house
crisscrossed with hidden mousetrails,
and under that a buried river
that seeps up through the cement
floor every spring,
and the tree roots snouting their slow way
into the drains;
under that, the bones
of our ancestors, or if not theirs, someone's,
mixed with a biomass of nematodes;
under that, bedrock, then molten
stone and the earth's fiery core;
and sideways, out into the city, street
and corner store and mall
and underpass, then barns and ruined woodlands, continent
and island, oceans, mists
of story drifting
on the tide like seaweed, animal
species crushed and blinking out,
and births and illnesses, hatred and love infra-
red, compassion fleshtone, prayer ultra-
violet; then rumours, alternate waves
of sad peace and sad war,
and then the air, and then the scintillating ions,
and then the stars. That's where
we are.

2.

Some centuries ago, when we lived at the edge
of the forest, on nights like this
you would have put on your pelt of a bear
and shambled off to prowl and hulk
among the trees, and be a silhouette of human
fears against the snowbank.
I would have chosen fox;
I liked the jokes,
the doubling back on my tracks,
and, let's face it, the theft.
Back then, I had many forms:
the sliding in and out
of my own slippery eelskin,
and yours as well; we were each other's
iridescent glove, the deft body
all sleight-of-hand and illusion.
Once we were lithe as pythons, quick
and silvery as herring, and we still are, momentarily,
except our knees hurt.
Right now we're content to huddle
under the shed feathers of duck and goose
as the wind pours like a river
we swim in by keeping still,
like trout in a current.
                                        Every cell
in our bodies has renewed itself
so many times since then, there's
not much left, my love,
of the originals. We're footprints
becoming limestone, or think of it
as coal becoming diamond. Less
flexible, but more condensed;
and no more scales or aliases,
at least on the outside. Though we've accumulated,
despite ourselves, other disguises:
you as a rumpled elephant-
hide suitcase with white fur,
me as a bramble bush. Well, the hair

was always difficult. Then there's
the eye problems: too close, too far, you're a blur.
I used to say I'd know you anywhere,
but it's getting harder.

3.

This is the solstice, the still point
of the sun, its cusp and midnight,
the year's threshold
and unlocking, where the past
lets go of and becomes the future;
the place of caught breath, the door
of a vanished house left ajar.

Taking hands like children
lost in a six-dimensional
forest, we step across.
The walls of the house fold themselves down,
and the house turns
itself inside out, as a tulip does
in its last full-blown moment, and our candle
flares up and goes out, and the only common
sense that remains to us is touch,

as it will be, later, some other
century, when we will seem to each other
even less what we were.

But the trick is just to hold on
through all appearances; and so we do,
and yes, I know it's you;
and that is what we will come to, sooner
or later, when it's even darker
than it is now, when the snow is colder,
when it's darkest and coldest
and candles are no longer any use to us
and the visibility is zero: *Yes.*
It's still you. It's still you.

MORNING IN THE BURNED HOUSE

In the burned house I am eating breakfast.
You understand there is no house, there is no breakfast,
yet here I am.

The spoon which was melted scrapes against
the bowl which was melted also.
No one else is around.

Where have they gone to, brother and sister,
mother and father? Off along the shore,
perhaps. Their clothes are still on the hangers,

their dishes piled beside the sink,
which is beside the woodstove
with its grate and sooty kettle,

every detail clear,
tin cup and rippled mirror.
The day is bright and songless,

the lake is blue, the forest watchful.
In the east a bank of cloud
rises up silently like dark bread.

I can see the swirls in the oilcloth,
I can see the flaws in the glass,
those flares where the sun hits them.

I can't see my own arms and legs
or know if this is a trap or blessing,
finding myself back here, where everything

in this house has long been over,
kettle and mirror, spoon and bowl,
including my own body,

including the body I had then,
including the body I have now
as I sit at this morning table, alone and happy,

bare child's feet on the scorched floorboards
(I can almost see)
in my burning clothes, the thin green shorts

and grubby yellow T-shirt
holding my cindery, non-existent,
radiant flesh. Incandescent.